ONCE MORE FROM EMMAUS

ONCE MORE FROM EMMAUS

Carlo Maria Martini

Translated
by
Matthew J. O'Connell

A Liturgical Press Book

 THE LITURGICAL PRESS
Collegeville, Minnesota

This book was published in Italian as *Ripartire da Emmaus,* © 1991 by Edizioni Piemme S.p.A., Via del Carmine 5, 15033 Casale Monferrato (AL), Italy.

1   2   3   4   5   6   7   8   9

Library of Congress Cataloging-in-Publication Data

Martini, Carlo M.
   [Ripartire da Emmaus. English]
   Once more from Emmaus / Carlo Maria Martini ; translated by Matthew J. O'Connell.
     p.   cm.
   Includes bibliographical references (p.).
   ISBN 0-8146-2158-9
   1. Evangelistic work.   2. Catholic Church—Missions.   I. Title.
BX2347.4.M3613   1995
266'.2—dc20   95-3530
                                                      CIP

Contents

Preface

In accordance with its pastoral plan for the year 1983–84 the diocese of St. Ambrose devoted itself to reflection on the *missionary* dimension that belongs to the very nature of the Church. In truth, the Church exists for the sake of mission; it exists to give witness to the world concerning the plan of salvation which God offers, in the person of the dead and risen Christ, to the men and women of every age. At that time the archbishop wrote a letter entitled "Departure from Emmaus" *(Partenza da Emmaus)* which was addressed chiefly to the pastoral workers of the diocese.

In succeeding years other pastoral programs were instituted, including one on charity ("Becoming a Neighbor"), which was the final step in the consideration of the intrinsic *being* of Christian community; and then one on *action*, specifically on the subjects of education and communication. This program is still being implemented.

Responding to some requests, the archbishop has since decided to emphasize the importance of the missionary element in the area of communication, since those who are given the gift of accepting the gospel cannot but feel a pressing need to communicate it to others.

To accomplish this, the archbishop returned his letter "Departure from Emmaus" in the form of a series of articles which appeared in the diocesan magazine *Il Segno* during 1990–91. He has entitled this series *Once More from Emmaus*. In these articles he makes the point, among others, that pastoral programs should be seen within a single whole, as different aspects of one reality—the Church—as it journeys toward the acquisition of the face which Christ, her Lord, asks her to make shine in the midst of the world.

It has seemed useful to collect these articles in a little volume so that readers may have easier access to them.

The Editors

Chapter 1

Yesterday evening, at a parish meeting, I listened for the umpteenth time to the question, "But what are we doing for the alienated, those who do not come to church? How can we say we are the Church if we do not live out the Church's mission, beginning with our own parish?"

The question always causes a certain discomfort, brings to the surface a secret malaise in the members of the parish council, a kind of vague sense of guilt. I myself succumb to a little impatience and shoot back, "But I've dealt with this at length in my letter 'Departure from Emmaus!' But then I feel obliged to add, "It is also true that that was the least understood of all my letters."

Then, however, I hear a voice within me asking, "What was it in that letter that should have been understood but was not? Why, despite the directives given in it, are there still so many misunderstandings and so many hesitations regarding the idea of the 'missionary Church'?" It rankles that so many of the baptized no longer come to church, and I would like to see them at Mass again. It grieves me that many seem to have forgotten that they are Christians. I would like to bring them back to the fold, even bring them back en masse, by some spectacular move. I grieve that these initiatives are not taken or, if they are, that they do not obtain the desired results. I ask myself, Are all these bitter and mournful thoughts really based on a correct idea of the Church's mission? Do they correspond to what the gospel of Jesus wants for our time? Probably only in part. The questions give voice to something that is true but at the same time to something that is not quite in order. I cannot in fact say that our communities are not ready to offer the means of salvation to those who ask for them. The number is increasing of those who have not been baptized (children whose parents put off their baptism, foreigners living among us) but who come to a point in life when they ask to be baptized. I know that these people are well received, that they receive personal attention from pastors as well as careful individual preparation, and so on.

Missing: An Enthusiastic Faith

What, then, do we mean when we lament, rightly, that the missionary spirit is lacking among us? We probably mean something more tenuous and yet essential. What is missing is the kind of enthusiastic faith that is contagious and that "could" bring the absent back to church and "help" those now Christian in name only to grow into an experiential Christianity. The missionary task within our Church must therefore be redefined as: An undertaking to revitalize the outlook of faith in those of the baptized who have become estranged.

The problem is thus much more difficult and complex. I am reminded of what the Letter to the Hebrews says: It is almost impossible for one who has tasted the waters of life and then fallen away to return and taste them again. Listen to the careful and terrifying words of this passage:

> It is impossible to restore again to repentance those who have once been enlightened, and have tasted the heavenly gift, and have shared in the Holy Spirit, and have tasted the goodness of the word of God and the powers of the age to come, and then have fallen away, since on their own they are crucifying again the Son of God and are holding him up to contempt. Ground that drinks up the rain falling on it repeatedly, and that produces a crop useful to those for whom it is cultivated, receives a blessing from God. But if it produces thorns and thistles, it is worthless and on the verge of being cursed; its end is to be burned over (Heb 6:4-8).

In other words, the problem here is the tragic crisis of *post-Christianity*, that is, of bringing back to a life of experiential faith those who were once to some extent initiated but who then fell away.

But this problem involves only a limited number of individuals, namely, those who until the age, let us say, of ten to fifteen have received an active Christian education (catechetical preparation for the sacraments, youth group, religious instruction in school, opportunities for a more intense Christian life in youth group and parish, and so on) but then have come to believe that these things have almost nothing to say to them or that the freer way in which they want to live is compatible with these surroundings and these religious practices. In the case of such individuals, it is possible to speak of an *alienation* from the faith. They always retain a certain nostalgia for it, and there is some possibility of their coming back (if only in connection with an engagement, a marriage, a first child, and so on). The problem here, then, is the problem of winning back to Christian practice those individuals who have tasted the faith to some extent.

But there is another category of persons among us: those who were simply baptized and then quickly "sacramentalized," in settings different from ours, without any careful preparation or any deeper catechesis, solely because it was the thing to do. The prevailing view in this class of persons, especially the men, is that churchgoing is for children and women. As adults, these men are contemptuous of overtures from the Church. They, too, need to be "brought back" to the faith, but in a somewhat different sense. For them Christianity has always been a matter of tradition, of priestly authority, of surviving rites from the past, of piousness and intolerable moral demands. In their case, those endeavoring to bring them back cannot count on a faith awareness that may be revived because this awareness was never there except in some extremely embryonic form. What is needed here is a reevangelization in the true and proper sense. But there is a major obstacle in the way: these people have turned their back on Christianity as outdated and irrelevant, too recondite and difficult, and even irksome.

This brief discussion shows that the problem is extremely difficult, and our communities cannot immediately take the blame if they find themselves somewhat embarrassed and with little to offer in the face of these realities.

These Thoughts Were Disregarded

Thus a simple question from a member of the parish council gave rise in me to a series of thoughts which for the moment I am unable to express or string together clearly. Once again, therefore, I am coming to the conclusion that I must rewrite my "Departure from Emmaus" *(Partenza da Emmaus)*!

In that letter I was endeavoring, along with the diocese, to face up to all these problems. As I now reread it attentively, I see that the essentials were already in it. Well, never mind, things turn out as they turn out. That year, 1983–84, there was a good deal to think about, in particular the centenary of St. Charles Borromeo, the Pope's second visit, and the pastoral efforts focused on the Bosto Arsizio Conference regarding the catechesis of adults (October, 1984), an activity rightly regarded as a "missionary" undertaking. Be that as it may, all the other basic thoughts of the letter have been in no small measure disregarded.

At a distance now of more than six years (the letter was dated July 7, 1983) and at the beginning of the final decade of the twentieth century, I think it important to try to rewrite that letter, section by section, as I rethink it in the light of more mature reflection—my own and that of the entire diocese—on the theme of "the internal missionary activity of the local Church," or, in other words, "concern for the *alienated.*" Those who wish to follow along with me will find in each issue of *Il Segno,* beginning with the next one, a short section of this rewritten letter, a draught of water, as it were, that can be drunk on the journey through the desert of modern unbelief and so revive the desire to be missionaries, to spread the gospel, starting in our own everyday situations here in Europe at the end of the twentieth century.

Il Segno 1 (January 1990)

Chapter 2

I have my entire diocese spread out before my [mind's] eye. I have been contemplating it in this way for ten years now. Almost countless markers, whether close in or in wider circles, remind me of the over one thousand parishes that are scattered across five provinces, from Lakes Maggiore and Como to the Milanese lowlands. I review and hear again their questions, their problems, their apprehensions; nor can I help making these my own. How could I do otherwise, when the Lord has told me: "This is your land, watch over it"?

Countless faces seem to scrutinize me persistently, down to my depths. Behind each gaze I sense a heart desirous of greater truth and justice, of the joy that comes with freedom and fellowship. My soul, too, the soul of a bishop, throbs and feels joy, struggles and hopes. And to each of these individuals I would like to cry out: "God is here, do not lose heart! You are not alone. And I, too, am near you." I think of each of you, my brother or my sister in the faith. And you who seek or doubt or are agnostic or an unbeliever—you, too, are present to me.

This evening is another evening heavy with deeply felt pain and deeply felt hope. Suddenly the words of Christ ring out: "I am with you all days, to the very end." The human race is not at the end of its rope. It has not reached its evening. Signs and premonitions on many sides give hope of an awakening. In any case, Christ always watches over us.

Yes, darkness and distress weigh down the human soul and at times almost kill it. Tragedies and calamities wipe the smile from our faces and make us choke on our tears. Others do not always seem to share very deeply in our sorrow; unfortunately, people get used even to the most alarming pieces of news, as they come like waves, each crashing on the one before it.

Christ's promise is there, as always, to give us confidence: Tomorrow a new day will dawn. Do not despair. Every evening will soon be matched by morning light. One evening long ago, as darkness fell on a long cherished expectation, two disciples were about to die the death of their ideals, the death of their great hope of a long-awaited liberator; for this hope had now vanished because of the accursed cross. "Which of us, Lord, has never experienced this death that afflicts the heart and spirit?"

"Stay with us, Lord, for it is almost evening . . ." (Luke 24:29)

On that evening of the great Easter day, even Emmaus felt the tremor of the resurrection. As the two disciples were breaking bread, Christ revealed the most tremendous news ever heard in human history: he is forevermore the risen one, the one who is eternally present. With him it is always day, and night brings no fear. The two disciples returned in haste to Jerusalem that they might tell of the joy of this unforgettable meeting.

"Which of us, Lord, has not had, at least once, the joy of meeting you, the risen one?" Is it not perhaps because of this daily exchange between our littleness and the power of the divine mystery that we reach the point of longing for a more just world, of feeling ourselves to be more fully brothers and sisters, and saying to everyone: He alone, the risen Christ, is the living bread we are to break, the Today that does not pass away?

And yet, after two thousand years, our human race seems still to be journeying toward Emmaus, like the two disciples, far from the saving cross, far from the hope of life, as though we were still living on that unending Easter day long ago. We go away silent and wearied, disappointed and deaf.

Even the eternal message of this most tangible of mysteries seems useless. It all seems stale and threadbare, a kind of impenetrable fog. Even the communities of believers are in this plight: wearied and disappointed by countless letdowns, they seem powerless at times in the face of the stubborn revolt of ancient idols. These idols are ready to recover and to present themselves again in a thousand different golden raiments. "What can be done, Lord? How to halt the spirit of evil? How to save the human race?"

Behold, Christ tells me once again today, this evening: "I need you. I need you to listen to me in all sincerity, with great faith. I am the Savior, and you must believe me. You must trust in the power of my love for this human race that I created and will to redeem. But I need your help, your participation. I need you, your arms, your heart, your mind. But you must be humble. The more you are at the disposal of my infinite love, the more effective you will be in working with me to save all created things." Christ wants me to play my part, and Christ wants you to play yours, dear brother and sister in the faith.

Let us return to Jerusalem. Let us set out again from Emmaus. Distractions and fatigue have estranged us and locked us up in our house in Emmaus, that is, in the little world of an apostolate reduced to the measure of our innate fears. We must set out to meet our brothers and sisters, those close to us and those we do not know, whether still faithful or already fleeing, and bear witness to them that Christ is alive, he is present here in our faith and in the joy of living in freedom of spirit, in our complete abandonment to the grace of God, in the absolute poverty of our human means.

Courage! Let us set out! The day is already waning, but Christ will give light for the road.

Listening to Jesus during a Missionary Journey
(see Matt 10:5-42)

I felt tired. Physically I was tired because of a long journey. More especially, my heart was full to overflowing with all that I had seen and come into close contact. Once again, on a "missionary" journey to areas overseas where the intolerable is part of daily life and not easily understood by foreigners, I was tempted to let myself by ruled by first impressions—those that assail us suddenly and elicit a chain of emotional but passing reactions.

I had not gone as a tourist. I wanted first and foremost to understand, to grapple with the Church there. I also intended to be there as an "evangelist." But how many questions and problems arose! What does it mean now, today, to evangelize? And what does it mean here among us, in our native place? I recollected myself and before falling asleep—for I needed sleep—it came to me spontaneously that I should pray a passage of the Gospels. I allowed the Lord to speak to me. Who better than he could inspire a correct judgment and make me smell the missionary fragrance of the genuine breath of the Spirit?

The Lord began by saying to me: "The text on which you are meditating is very demanding. It is, in summary form, an entire program of missionary apostolate. My beloved Matthew has brought together, in what you call chapter ten of his Gospel, the pieces of advice, counsels, directives, which I gave to my disciples on various occasions and in varying circumstances. It is so important a program that it became for the first community of believers an indispensable point of reference and a daily examination of conscience in which they could all take part."

"For what reason?" I interjected.

"Perhaps never so much as on these missionary visits have you, my beloved disciple, felt the thrill of the superabundant harvest and of the masses which seem, like shipwrecked sailors, to be at the mercy of every human tempest. On the other hand, is there not a need, even in your immense diocese, of more workers to serve in my kingdom? Then, too, is it not true that the eyes of the servants of my word are not always watchful, attentive, far-sighted, and prophetic? These servants are satisfied at times to hold tightly to a few grains of corn and are unwilling really to see the grain turning golden in limitless fields with their promise of hope."

"Yes, Lord, that is so!"

"There's something I want to say to you now, and it is the answer to my first question. It is I, the Lord, who chooses workers for my kingdom. I choose as I will, and I choose also for the sake of the faith of Christians—a faith in which priestly and religious vocations grow and mature. That is why you ought to pray and beseech me constantly. Is not the fact that I myself choose my collaborators a sign of my great respect for human freedom? If I have called you to work with me and for me, it is because I have great confidence in your freedom. Of that freedom you must render an account to me. The kingdom is built up by my grace and your human freedom."

"Great is your love, my God, and great my responsibility! It is here, in this dialogue between God and human beings, that your kingdom begins!"

"Look, what does my free choice imply? That each person can do as he or she thinks fit? That each person called is to work for their own profit? Disciples are disciples if they listen to their teacher. Disciples are faithful to me if they listen and act, if they keep my word and put it into practice, consciously and with interior freedom. The freer they become interiorly, the more open and docile they are to my grace. If I call, there is but one response: to do what I myself did first, as I did it, and together with me. It is not enough to know what I did and how I did it. It is necessary to do it daily. This will demand renunciation and struggle from my disciples. Such is the calling of one who takes my cross seriously and follows me daily."

"How hard that is, Lord!"

"This is what I ask of all true disciples. You must have trust and obey me! I came into the midst of humanity to say clearly to each of you: This is how you too must act if we are to join in saving the human race. No one can be my disciple and disregard what I did. Those who work on their own, as though I had little or no part to play, cannot call themselves my collaborators. When I sent the Twelve on their mission, I did not give them a long list of things they were to say. Instead I emphasized the behavior that should mark them on their journey from town to town among the people. During these last days you have seen wretched surroundings, emaciated faces, crowds of pitiful folk who are among the poorest in the world."

"I shall never be able to forget them, Lord!"

"I have shared the hard labor of my faithful missionaries. I have seen the weariness and worry on their faces and read in their hearts the joy they experienced as they proclaimed the freedom of the kingdom of God. They have chosen to live among the people and with the people, to share their suffering, to urge them daily to keep on hoping. Ordinary people can recognize the presence of a true father, of one who sincerely wills their good, who tells no lies and will not betray them. They understand that the missionary is truthful because they see and touch the tangible presence of a love that reaches to the heart of each individual. The gaze fixed by preference on the weakest is already the best witness to the mercy of God. Words count to the extent that they find expression in actions and a consistent life."

"There is only one word that really counts, Lord! Your word, made flesh."

"These humble servants and friends of mine have grasped the most important thing: it is the manner of life that, above all else, makes a disciple credible and worthy of respect. And what is this apostolic manner of life if not the simple, poor, self-less activity of the gospel?: Tenderness to the weak, strength to the stubborn, no compromises with those in power, a heart full of trust in the goodness of God and in his unpredictable providence. Use this world's goods sparingly, cautiously, prudently, as means and nothing more. As God's gifts that keep the heart free."

"This wisdom of yours is true wisdom, Lord!"

"I see that you have been deeply impressed by the great poverty of these dear missionaries of mine, by their limitless generosity, their strong and courageous spirit, their utter giving of themselves to everyone without exception. A soul is worth more than anything else whatsoever. Every soul is to be loved and served sincerely, selflessly, and without demanding

11

a return. Freely given service is especially pleasing to me, for gratuitousness is the mark of my own divine self! Disinterested service is the most beautiful characteristic of any vocation. Are we not called to give freely what we have received as a gift from God?"

What shadows lie upon our service! God's selfless giving should cause us uneasiness and be our daily goad. But the objection can be raised: Yes, these missionaries are certainly to be admired. In them we see the great work being accomplished by the Spirit who breathes where and as he wills, especially wherever the proclamation of the liberating and saving message is most urgently needed. But nowadays we have the impression that it is in the so-called Third World that hearts are more docile to receive this message. Furthermore—the objection continues—is it not possible that the very environment in which missionaries are working is a stimulus to their witness? Is not life among the poor a strong stimulus to those called, since in these circumstances they feel an urgent need to live a consistent life of solidarity? The people themselves thus will receive and lay hold of the apostles they need. Missionaries will either live in solidarity or be forced to return home.

Meanwhile, here at home, in our country that is so rich in age-old traditions, yes, here among us who live amid people of little faith and even less practice, people tossed to and fro by countless temptations to materialism and torn between a self that regards itself as Christian and a self that justifies permissiveness of every kind—here at home we must ask ourselves: Is it not easier for us ministers of Christ and for any committed Christians to be overcome by fear and to withdraw into ourselves? Or else to try a few letters and, after the first failure, to turn passive and live in calm resignation? Or else to flee elsewhere, to some distant place, to one or another mission country, in search of an escape?

How, then, are we to live and proclaim the gospel here in this blessed house of ours, where the sun that rises for us grows paler day by day and we feel the heaviness of an air that is increasingly unbreathable; where a bit of progress today spurs us to frenetic activity or else drives away those who cannot go at a steady pace and relegates them to bitter isolation? How are we to confront this obsessive attitude to life that seems to be trying to infect even the most alert spirits, and how are we to restore in our brothers and sisters personality and conscience, soul and interior freedom, a will to do good and a creative responsibility?

[The Lord responds:] "I have listened carefully to your outburst, which expresses the feelings of not a few, and, to tell the truth, I see good reasons for your suffering. For the moment I shall limit myself to saying that in every place the reign of God comes to maturity amid difficulties and tribulations, hindrances and dissensions of every kind. Every kind of ground is hard in its own way, and the seed has trouble taking root. Tears alone can soften the soil and make it workable. Rather than the fortuitous physical characteristics of the soil, it is the weeds or grasses that make it resistant. And this not only during the time of growth but even during the harvest! Yet you, a human being and my creature, are unfortunately capable of struggling for a sun that is denied you and rain that is less acid (though I harrow you as hard as I can) and then at the harvest of keeping the weeds and burning the grain. But I shall never forget you, my beloved disciple, no matter where you are. You are not alone! You are not sowing by yourself, for it is [my] word that saves. Trust in me and in my unfailing patience. I am there, in every corner of the earth and of your heart. The stronger the human hardness of heart, the greater [my] Father's love. [Am I] not the one who works miracles at every moment? [My] desire for the good of creation is too great for [me] to leave this creation in the hands of the Evil One. [My] Spirit stands watch day and night, and asks for greater faith and courage!"

"'Greater faith and courage!' These words of yours, Lord, have remained in my heart. I shall be returning to them shortly."

Il Segno 2 (February 1990)

Chapter 3

Before continuing our journey let us catch our breath for a moment and reflect on what was said in the previous installment. That installment dealt with numbers 8 and 9 of "Departure from Emmaus" and referred back to two passages of the Gospels: the disciples at Emmaus (Luke 24:13-35) and the missionary discourse of Jesus (Matt 10). The key themes were *freedom* and *way of life*.

A Look Back

Human Freedom Cross-pollinated by the Risen Jesus

The missionary life is not undertaken on our own initiative, but is the consequence of the command given by the risen Jesus. Jesus comes to meet our uncertain and purposeless freedom and assigns it a task. Our freedom springs to life at his word and courageously embarks on the journey to a mission. What I mean is that the renewal of our missionary undertaking, even "at home" (that is, within the confines of our parishes and the diocese), is not the fruit of a heroic or individual decision of a few; it is simply the fruit of an authentic encounter with the risen Jesus. Apart from this there are only velleities, the conjuring up of abstract and ineffective projects, sterility and lamentation.

Way of Life

A missionary life is not an abstraction. Missionaries live in the field. It is very useful at this point to take as a model true missionaries, especially those who are in the poorest countries of the world. It is, above all else, their humble way of life, their closeness to the people, their sharing with them, their selflessness that qualifies them. This is what Jesus says in Matthew 10. In this chapter he puts the emphasis not on what the disciples are to say but on their manner, their way of life. We often forget this and we ask all sorts of questions about what we are to say, about how the message is to be translated into the language of our day, about how we are to overcome the alienness of the culture we bring with us, and so on. But matters are much simpler. Our starting point must be an "evangelical" way of life. The gospel is preached first and foremost through a simple, selfless, open, and courteous way of life. St. Francis of Assisi kept this lesson in mind and was most effective.

The two ideas of *freedom* and *way of life* play a controlling role throughout the letter "Departure from Emmaus" and are indeed the key to it. Our moving quickly beyond them to the question of what to say or what works to undertake is as it were the worm that continually eats away at our missionary energies and reduces them to sterile velleities. Let us not forget this point as the present letter unfolds.

Let us turn now to a rereading of the pages of "Departure from Emmaus" in which I commented on the discourses of Jesus after the Last Supper, as reported in John 13–17, and on the missionary mandate in Matthew 28:16-20.

"I shall not leave you orphans; I shall come back to you" (John 14:18)

These pages of the Gospel of John are extraordinarily rich and fascinating, despite their seeming wordiness and to some extent repetitiveness. But does not this symphony have a motif that recurs in various movements? Indeed, and the motif is love. It is repeated over and over in a series of words and images.

Christ is present, about to say farewell to his disciples. Sadness and melancholy are etched on the faces of the disciples.

But Christ is journeying beyond death. His words overcome human barriers and re-create all of creation. Here and everywhere, yesterday, today, and tomorrow.

Christ is here, today, and he says to me, "You are my presence in the world. I live in you. I was dead and I rose and I returned to my Father so that you might be able to continue my mission of salvation in this present world which you see and touch today, in all its experience of struggle and expectation, of decline and hope. The world, moreover, is not made up simply of souls. The world is also society's customs and mindsets focused on death rather than life, and its harmful power structures. Such is the world in which you must bear witness to me. My disciples are those who struggle to save the whole of creation, for that is what my Father willed and that is the mission he entrusted to me. To save means to rescue the human conscience from its enslavement to evil. It means to restore breath to all living things by wresting them from the grip of the Evil One."

"Lord, it is no simple matter for any human being to escape this spiral. Moreover, your disciples sometimes feel that they are all alone. Your farewell at the Supper still feels to them like a definitive departure. And yet, as soon as your words enter our hearts, we feel your promise renewed: 'I will not leave you orphans!' And the certainty of your words is always with us: 'Take courage, I have overcome the world!'"

A Symbolic Gesture (John 13:1-20)

John records an action of Jesus at the Last Supper that has great symbolic power. All the more so, because the Master shows himself in the garb of a servant. The washing of the disciples' feet conveys the real message, the authentically new thing, in the institution of the Eucharist (which the fourth evangelist does not mention). God has stooped to us, humbling himself to the utmost. And yet we are reluctant at times to dirty the hem of our garment in saving our brothers and sisters who suffer loneliness and hardship, marginalization and the various forms of social leprosy.

Christ wants us to be like him, and this not simply by doing one or another act of charity, however praiseworthy. We must feel ourselves united to him as the branch to the vine.

"Rightly, Lord, did the saints experience the thrill of infinity when they thought of dwelling in God one and three, in a God who is Love. Grant, Lord, that we may embody a little of your mystery of unity and everlasting love. The love we bring with us on every road and every wavelength is a sign of your love as Father, Son, and Holy Spirit. Lord Jesus, you want us to be able with your help to manifest fully your universal love. You want us, who are believers in the Absolute, to love our brothers and sisters without reserve, whatever their color. Our responsibility is great, but you, God, are greater still, for nothing is impossible to you. At times you ask of us but a little speck of faith and a mere puff of courage."

Go and Teach All Nations (Matt 28:19)

An elderly missionary was talking to me. His words were words of wisdom, for they came from a heart that had never wearied of loving his people and hoping for their good. I listened, and my mind's eye saw a series of visions of the risen Jesus. Rightly so, for there was a connection between the confidence of this missionary and the words of the Teacher to his disciples.

"Your Eminence," this friend began, "my soul is filled with a constant longing: to succeed in telling everyone that Jesus is the only redeemer. There are still millions and millions of men and women who do not know that they have a heavenly Father who loves them all and wills that all be saved.

"But after all—I ask myself—what more could I do than I have chosen to do? I am present to a poor people who yearn for a liberator. The problem that distresses me is how best to proclaim the message of Christ to this people whose cultures and way of life are so different from those of our Western world.

"It was not easy for me at the beginning, at their first impact on me, to understand and accept the customs and mentality of this people of mine. Accustomed as I was to live in a certain way that had now become part of me, I was tempted to confuse culture and faith and to transmit the one along with the other. I labored hard to lay hold of the real substance of the Christian mystery and to give it flesh and blood in the historical reality and authentic social traditions of this people. Was not the important thing to help concrete human beings reach interior freedom and authenticity, while allowing them to continue living in their de facto environment? What mistakes I made!"

I wanted to interrupt the man, but I allowed him to continue. I did not want to embitter him still more with my philosophical and theological distinctions.

"Christ did not tell us: Go and bring 'your' faith to all nations! No, he ordered us to announce 'his' gospel! Christ did not tell us: Go out into the entire world and make converts to the Christian cause, so as to increase its prestige and power! Nor did he say: Take my gospel and adapt it as you see fit so that each people may use and consume it! This last is a serious danger today, not only in mission countries but especially in our own Europe, where the claim has been made, in the name of progress—of course!—that Christianity must be reduced to permissiveness.

"People here, your Eminence, are capable of understanding why we wish them well and why we have come from afar off to announce the good news to them. These people are able to distinguish between all the harm the colonizers did and all the good the Church has done for them, at times even staining their soil with the blood of its martyrs."

This elderly missionary was speaking passionately in behalf of his land; he wanted confirmation, as it were, of his already heroic ministry, a greater acknowledgment of his duty to continue living in those regions where for years now he had felt himself to be "one of them."

On his face I also read a question that was making him both uneasy and curious, that was a thorn in his side but at the same time had to do with his very reason for being what he was: In what does the revolutionary power of Christ consist? What is the secret of making this power operate more effectively to unsettle and renew?

Indeed, Jesus represents the authentic truth of every human being. He is the true new Human Being. No one can any longer do without him. This is the main truth to be proclaimed to any and every people, in every corner of the earth.

Il Segno 3 (March 1990)

Chapter 4

Let me review briefly our progress thus far. I have been endeavoring to reflect on nos. 10 and 11 of my earlier letter, which were sections of chapter 2, entitled "The Message." The purpose of that chapter was to set down the message contained in some fundamentally important passages of the New Testament. Thus far I have reviewed here the meeting of Jesus with the disciples at Emmaus (Luke 24:13-35), the missionary discourse (Matt 10), the discourses after the Last Supper (John 13–17), and the great missionary mandate (Matt 28:16-20 and parallels). From each of these passages I have tried to pick out what seems to me to be essential from our point of view. In the passage about Emmaus the theme is the weak and indecisive human freedom which Jesus arouses and renders capable of missionary proclamation. In Matthew 10 the focus is on the evangelical life style, which is the first message that a missionary conveys to others. John 13–17 tell of the new way in which Jesus is present in a difficult and hostile world: he nows acts through disciples who are one with him and prolong his humble, loving presence. In the great missionary mandate (Matt 28:16-20) the key point is the certainty that Jesus is salvation for every human being and every culture.

I shall go on now to the conclusion of the chapter entitled "The Message" and reread its final section (no. 12 of "Departure from Emmaus"). It reminds us of the missionary vitality of the early Christians as we see it in the Acts of the Apostles and the letters of St. Paul.

The First Missionary Communities

Have any of you ever visited the places where the early Christian communities were located, or retraced the journeys of St. Paul? The experience leaves an indelible impression. One seems to feel in the air the joy of the very early communities, to hear their festive songs and sense their missionary enthusiasm. But, apart from such an experience, the word of God itself, as found in the Book of Acts and the letters of St. Paul, should be enough to bring to life again for us the enthusiastic faith of the first Christians. The Book of Acts has always thrilled me. Even a child can grasp the great works of God that are told in it and understand the heroic fidelity of his witnesses. As the years passed, I became increasingly fascinated by the overwhelming power of the gospel as expressed in Paul's preaching and letters. I gradually discovered the secret of these most precious New Testament books. They document the mighty, irresistible progress of the preaching of the risen Christ.

The Acts of the Apostles provide splendid material for contemplating, in faith, the mystery of the redeemer, as this impresses and fascinates individuals and countries, cities and peoples of every color, transcending nationalist barriers, political factions, and racial prejudices, and overturning social hierarchies in the name of the radical, inherent dignity of every person.

During one of my pastoral visitations a young person asked me: "Your Eminence, what drove the first Christian community to bear witness to the gospel with such enchanting enthusiasm, so that the good news spread throughout the then known world in a short time?" The question might also have been intended as a provocation: Are not some religious sects spreading far and wide today?

I answered: "I am convinced that the first Christians were driven not by an emotional enthusiasm or a spirit of proselytism but rather by a strong, clear-sighted, lively missionary consciousness."

The young person said: "Then the only goal of the early Church was to bear witness to the gospel and proclaim it to all, with no one excluded?"

"Definitely!" I replied. "To them Christ embodied the certainty of truth and universal salvation and liberation, precisely because he is the savior and liberator of every person. The Church of the early days felt obliged, by its very faith, to spread the gospel; it was conscious, strongly conscious, of being a mother, in Christ, to every living being. Christianity spread, therefore, as a result of the Church's self-consciousness."

Another young person spoke up: "This means that now as in the past the Church of Christ does not depend for its life on various structures and strategies, but that the latter, which have evolved over the centuries, are simply the visible expression of the innate vitality of the Church itself. In other words, the Church spreads precisely because it is alive."

I tried to explain: "Certainly, the Church can by no means remain a small-scale society and build itself a kingdom of security and privilege. It does indeed rely also on structures, but above all it must have a clear consciousness of being witness to Christ and must strive to reach its sole true goal, namely, the real salvation of the human race."

But another young person insisted: "How is it, then, that today, in the more industrialized countries, the countries with ancient traditions of faith, we seem to be seeing a worrisome growth of indifference? Are the Church's disciples losing the true image of the Church? Is the Church's missionary consciousness on the decline? Is that perhaps the reason—I mean the decline in a personal awareness that we are meant to be bold believers—why we find Christians following an inconsistent, individualistic, and worldly way of life? As a result, they live on the fringes, away from the spring of living water, and dwell in the desert. Ought we to wish for periods of tension and struggle, persecution and hostility, so that a genuine, courageous, and exemplary faith may be awakened in us?"

I replied: "Even today we are already in such a time of struggle, although many do not realize it. And the Church is only at the beginning of her journey. What are two thousand years when compared with the almost two thousand million years still ahead of us? The universe has unexpected resources, new flashes of light on the horizon, and new seeds of hope where the soil has for centuries been thought barren, an undeveloped wilderness, a sandy desert. Even here and now new buds are appearing in our midst; after the winter spring will soon be here."

As for the first Christians, it was their concrete way of life itself that became "missionary." The same will be true in our time. Real Christians, authentic ecclesial communities, will be able to rouse admiration, respect, dialogue, and conversion.

Persecutions may also come, as in the time of the early martyrs, and in fact they are already going on in various parts of the world. But that will only spur Christians to emerge from their own little world and enter everywhere into unforeseen contexts, areas previously unknown, and hearts that await truth and justice.

Was not the Church at its beginning driven by persecutions to go forth and proclaim the gospel elsewhere? Thus began an evangelization that spread ever further, in any and every setting, in any and every set of circumstances. It made its way through daily contact with all peoples, even in prison. In the darkness of the prison at Philippi "Paul and Silas were praying and singing hymns to God, and the prisoners were listening to them" (Acts 16:25).

When a group of laypersons were alarmed at the continued existence of quarrels in their community, I had to tell them that the early Church had a secret: they faced up to their own numerous conflicts, internal and external, with a great determination born of their faith in the risen Christ. Thus they related all problems to the heart of the Christian mystery. It is in the same perspective that [churches today] must resolve all tensions; it is in the mystery of Christ that they must try to settle the usual misunderstandings that arise between groups and movements. It is the missionary dimension that makes a parochial community grow; only so can a community overcome emotionalism and jealousies, gossip and parochialism. How many expectations would then receive an adequate answer! There would be new responses to strengthen communities that are in decline or have settled for self-satisfaction!

Christ asks us to have greater faith and courage! And the Church urges us to draw strength and inspiration from a rereading of the Acts of the Apostles and the letters of St. Paul. I remind you here of two passages in particular, which I already have suggested to you in "Departure from Emmaus": the passage in which Paul speaks of his desire to spend his life proclaiming the gospel, but at the same time says that his great love of the Lord makes him want to die and meet him (Phil 1:21-25); and the passage in which the life of the first believers is described as having roused in others the desire to become members of this community (Acts 2:42-47; 4:32-37). It is from such passages as these that we ought, by the power of the Holy Spirit, to draw faith and the courage to proclaim the gospel.

Il Segno 4 (April 1990)

Chapter 5

We have thus far been rereading together the first part of the letter entitled "Departure from Emmaus." This first part is titled "The Message." Its purpose is to summarize the missionary message that emerges from some passages of the New Testament.

We shall now begin to reread the second part of that pastoral letter, entitled "The Disparity." Its purpose is to make us think about the gap between the missionary ideal of the New Testament and the missionary reality in our communities. It is intended also to provide help in bridging this gap so that it will not be simply a burden laid on us to produce only a painful sense of an impossible task. Our need is to come to grips successfully with the situation described in the Gospel stories of the multiplication of the loaves, where the disciples, being asked to feed so many people, answer: "Are we to go and buy two hundred denarii worth of bread, and give it to them to eat?" (Mark 6:37). How are we to move beyond such attitudes?

"We have nothing here but five loaves and two fishes" (Matt 14:17)

Once again, although perhaps more intensely than usual, I was feeling [as I wrote "The Disparity"] the tension, almost the direct conflict, between needs and resources in the varied situations throughout this dear territory that belongs to St. Ambrose.

The people of God here are squeezed in a vise: the one jaw is all the new undertakings required by new needs, and the other is the existing programs that must not be neglected.

Well (I said to myself that weekend), everyone wants the good of the community. But some who seek it are weighed down by fear of novelty; others live in utopian dreams; still others, who are in the majority, flounder in midstream. And you, Lord, what are you doing to help us?

I was struck by a typically youthful statement at one of my meetings with the leaders of parish communities: "Look, Your Eminence, because they are fearful of anything new, people in our community have continued to hold on for dear life to what they already have, and now nothing remains but habits left over from the past!" But another rebutted the charge: "No! Some individuals want too much change, and the people do not follow them!"

In the final analysis, did not both parties have the same pastoral longing?

In any case, it does no good any longer to bar the doors and windows of the house in order to prevent the influence of a stubborn materialism that in the guise of deceitful promises affects every breath human beings take. Our communities cannot escape reality, be it tragic or seductive. They are part of it. They are a plot of ground on which we must live, a part of this earth which, as the Bible tells us, will always be to some extent cursed and will always be witness to a message of hope. We must remain where we are, then, and each of us must daily win our freedom by the sweat of our brow. This is our duty: to give each person the freedom of Christ, the freedom that liberates the heart.

Structures, environments, and institutions certainly have their part to play, provided only that they help persons of faith to grow and make others grow. But what are we to do when faced with the onrush of uncontrollable situations that suffocate and squeeze and oppress us? I would like to help those who ask this painful question by making them aware of Christ's great love and his limitless patience and of how he died, defeated and on a cross, only to rise again and promise that he would forever be really, totally present to us with his irresistible power to conquer every evil.

There is no doubt that life in today's world brings daily crises. The demands made on us are numerous and insistent, and seem never ending; how can we respond to all of them? There is no time even to listen to them. At times we don't even have the desire to listen, since the means available are what we see, and our own limitations account for the rest.

On the other hand, if we are disciples of Christ, how can we sleep in peace while leaving each individual to carry his or her burden and the weak to fall by the way? We have only five loaves and two fishes. What then can we do for such a mass of people? Are we perhaps to go and buy bread for all of them? How? With what money, and from whom? "Would it not be better, Lord, to send the crowd away?"

John the Evangelist understands that I, too, am confused, and he bids me pay attention to one sentence in his narrative: "Jesus knew well what he was going to do, but he said this in order to test Philip" (John 6:6). "How true it is, Christ, that your gospel will never cease to amaze us!"

The Lord allowed the disciples to speak their mind and to find every excuse for resolving the situation in the most logical way, namely, by sending the crowd away. That would have been my answer as well. But then they were led to understand things in the light of the Holy Spirit.

Christ alerts us too, us Christians two thousand years later: "Be attentive! Every situation is a 'test.' And if you have the wisdom to make out its meaning, you will be able to overcome any difficulties, especially those in which your essential vocation is involved."

When Christ told the apostles, "You give them something to eat" (Matt 14:16), he certainly did not expect a superhuman response from them but was looking rather for an act of faith in him. This was the "test": the disciples should have been aware of their limitations, their timidity, their inability to handle the present situation, and should have had complete trust in the Master: trust in his word, in his saving works, in his merciful power. And they should have obeyed!

That is the authoritative answer to our problem! Every urgent need that challenges us in our missionary vocation is a test that puts us in our right place and makes us humbly aware of the absolute claim of the gospel. Humility and obedience to Christ—these make the disciple and are the sign of the disciple's authenticity. Consequently, they are also the source of the disciple's extraordinary courage. Humility makes us conscious of what we are, and obedience places us in the hands of divine providence. Humility makes us conscious realists. Obedience gives us courage and even recklessness when this is required, for it rids us of chronic fears, facile illusions, and comfortable resignation. "Why should we be afraid, Christ, when we are with you?"

"A new teaching—with authority" (Mark 1:27)

If I had to attend to every question asked of me and attempt a response to each, I would have time for nothing else. What, then, is the best pedagogical tactic in the situation? Would it not be enough to establish a basic principle or, if we prefer, some key truths, by which to resolve doubts and enable us to capture the reflection of the divine light that clarifies everything and makes everything converge on the mystery of the risen Christ?

As we read the Gospels we discover how the people who hear Jesus remain fascinated by him. Why was this? "He taught them as one having authority, and not as the scribes" (Mark 1:22). Or again: "What is this? A new teaching—with authority," to cite the exclamation which all those present at the miracle of the demoniac utter in their amazement (Mark 1:27).

The authority they perceive is unique, exceptional, proper to the Son of God who came among us to reveal the face of the Father. Christ alone could fully reveal the Father's face, because he embodies all of God's love for humankind. This is why Christ said of himself: "I am the way, the truth, and the life" (John 14:6). Moreover, this authority of the Son of God is the basis for all the activity of the incarnate Word and for all the human experience embodied in his words, his choices, his decisions; in his calling of the disciples, his institution of the sacraments, and his establishment of the Church as the means by which God's salvation is communicated to human beings. This authority of Christ is not something unrelated to historical events, but on the contrary reaches out to all realities of all ages with their most hidden implications and to all structures and contexts, even to the outermost limits of creation: to the known and the still to be known, the unfolding of the centuries and the irresistible advance of history.

"Even today, Christ, you speak with authority in the mission of your disciples." Here is where each person's responsibility comes into play—mine, too. Woe to us if we betray this authority of Christ! Our mission, in its every aspect, its every action, its every word, cannot fail to be marked by at least a spark of this extraordinary divine energy.

I was silent in contemplation before the crucified Christ. He alone could inspire me to something great. "Speak to me, God! I want no other word but yours! Your word, God, would immediately bring light into every darkness, and any human being would become free. Why do you not speak it? Yes, I know, you want me to play my part. You are waiting for me to struggle and search, so that every gift may become a light for those who do not yet see."

"That is true, my disciple. You have my word: why do you not speak it? You have my light: why do you not spread it? I have given you my life: why do you hold on to it jealously? You have the gift of faith, the greatest gift a human being can have. It is the gift that gives itself. You cannot hold it close and keep it only for yourself. Faith is a certitude that shines out and cannot but be enthusiastic. It is joy springing from a discovery that cannot be kept hidden. Do you who believe realize that you are not alone? You have my presence, which is mysterious, yes, but real. More real than the presence in any human dialogue. You have my Church, in which each individual has a special vocation to do my will. But to do it with others, as a

Church: in the variety and multiplicity of charisms and in a union of intentions for the better service of each of my children according to his or her own truest identity. My Church is compounded of grace and human weaknesses, saints and structures, charisms and rituals. It is for this reason that I ask of you the obedience of faith. Obedience to my merciful love, to my fullest generosity. You must be on guard not to betray my grace through human compromises. You must be humble and critical regarding your own limitations, but on the other hand you must not let yourself be overcome by the dross of time. See to it, rather, that the rites, institutions, and traditions of the Church's life are docilely brought into accordance with the Spirit, so that you avoid the danger of obscuring or restraining the course of my grace."

"How am I to succeed in this, Lord? I feel not so much doubt as fear and great anxiety. Every one of your disciples has his or her limitations, and suffers from them."

"Behold, I am with you. The Church is with you. And you have effective means at hand, tools that will make any human power fade from view: my grace, redemption, the gift of the risen life. What more do you want? You must lead people to understand that in the mystery of the cross everyone is accepted, loved, forgiven, and saved. To succeed in this you must start with the concrete reality of each of your brothers and sisters. You must understand them and enter into dialogue with them—with great prudence, sensitivity, and attention, without rejecting them because of their errors. Listen and understand, and then open up new perspectives for them, horizons of hopes that are surer and humanly richer, and instill in them a longing for the infinite. Are you discouraged? But don't you sense the joy of such an extraordinary undertaking?"

The Lord's message for me and my diocese is clear. What do these committed communities of mine really need, especially today? They need a great ability to read every event and every human situation in the light of Christ's gospel.

The Lord asks of us a profound interior docility to his word and a keen attention to human reality, along with the courage to censure, if need be, errors, sins, injustices, and inconsistencies, and with a strong love of our brothers and sisters, a love that does not crush any desire they may have of what is good, any effort at sincere dialogue, or any human anxiety, wherever these may be found.

Our struggle has but one goal: to lead everyone to hope of a new day: the day of the resurrection of Christ!

With only five loaves and two fishes, or perhaps even less, we feel ourselves to be really poor. But woe to us if we think that by having or desiring more, we will do away with all problems. Any collision with reality is a test, and disciples, even though they suffer from it, must face it without fear, trusting as they do in the grace of Christ.

"Lord, you want us to have a healthy realism and great humility. The difficulties are there on my way of the cross; I cannot pretend they are not. Few or many, they cause suffering to a heart that loves. Lord, grant me eyes that see clearly and a heart that is pure. Pastoral tensions must be faced in all their complexity and urgency, as we walk together as friends, looking one another in the face, with respect, extending a hand to one another, and seeking counsel even from those we may judge to be poorer than ourselves.

"And you, Lord, urge a spirit of forgiveness on us who often betray your limitless fatherly heart by our resentments and the arrogance shown by the elder brother of the parable. We are pitiless toward those already outside, while at home we deal harshly with those who err and go away. We believers do not always understand one another; we even prefer not to understand one another but each to stay in our own little group."

The gospel demands that we train ourselves to forgive, and each community must be disposed to be on its knees in the confessional which is the Church of Christ. We cannot walk together if we do not forgive one another or if we reject fraternal correction—that act of charity that trains us to be humble, to repent of our ways, and to engage in frank dialogue. To ask and give forgiveness: is this not the primary proof of the newness of the gospel? And is not the gift of the Father's mercy the new thing which Christ brings?

"You ask everything of us, Jesus: the few loaves we have, and whatever we are. You in turn are quick to multiply our littleness by your saving love. You ask of us the little we have—and you want everything—in an interior dialogue the words of which are eternal. We feel your breath in us, and we thank you. Be here with us in all your mystery, and let our souls feel the ardor and hope your presence inspires, in the simplicity of children asleep in their mothers' arms."

Il Segno 5 (May, 1990)

Chapter 6

During meetings or retreats I often find myself being challenged: "Well, then, what ought we to do?"

The question reflects a mind alarmed and uncertain, but also a desire for guidelines and remedies with which to revitalize the amorphous mass of faith around us—as though this revitalization depended on some great plan for strategic action.

"He appointed twelve . . . to be with him . . ." (Mark 3:14)

"What are we to do?" Each time I hear this question my pastor's soul feels uneasy, for I am aware that the question is badly put and that the very asking of it shows how far people are from the heart of the problem.

Luke writes that crowds of ordinary people as well as groups of tax collectors and soldiers hastened to hear the Baptist preach and then asked him what they were to do. John, Luke tells us, did not refuse an answer but urged each group to act in ways worthy of those who have been converted. This is certainly a first step. What more can be expected?

But two disciples of the precursor did ask for more on the day when, hearing John speak of Jesus as he was passing by, they decided to follow Jesus. And when Jesus asked them, "What are you looking for?" they answered, "Rabbi, where are you staying?" John the Evangelist then tells us: "They came and saw where he was staying, and they remained with him that day. It was about four o'clock in the afternoon" (John 1:39).

"Teacher, where are you staying?" (this seems to us a natural answer), and Jesus allowed them to remain with him for a few hours that afternoon: a few hours of intense contemplative joy. Jesus spoke to them, and his gaze was impressed on their hearts. They seemed to be living outside of time. The words from eternity which they heard remained their secret; when Andrew later met his brother Peter, he managed to say only: "We have found the Messiah!" and he brought Simon to Jesus (John 1:41-42).

John the Evangelist would never forget the precise time—four in the afternoon—or the details of the meeting, although he could find no better way of expressing it than to say "they remained with him." [I hear him saying:] "The important thing to us was not to know where the Teacher was staying, but rather to remain with him. By remaining we discovered his extraordinary personality, the fascination of his gaze, the truthfulness of his words. A mystery entered into us, and we were irresistibly drawn. The house we entered were suddenly acquired different dimensions—it was outside time and space."

It was not only these two disciples, Andrew and John, who were given this privilege; Jesus gave all of the Twelve similar moments of intense communion.

Consider how meaningful Mark's words are: "He appointed twelve that they might be with him and be sent out to preach and have power to expel demons" (Mark 3:13-14). And, in fact, did not the entire public life of Jesus involve a "being with" his disciples?

"There are no better words to describe a moment of contemplative rest, and it is here, in this divine respite, that our spirits tremble with desire for you, eternal Word."

"What ought we to do?" The question echoes uneasily within me, because of the short-sighted anxieties it displays.

How could we have forgotten our early pastoral programs, with their progressive invitations to enter the *contemplative dimension of life,* to meditate on the source— "In the beginning was the Word"—and to let ourselves be captivated by the irresistible words "I will draw all to myself"?

"How often, like the divine Teacher, I have wanted to *be with* you, my dear faithful and sharers in my calling, so that I might get to know you more fully, confide to you my pastoral anxieties and at the same time lighten yours, and so feel united with one another by Christ's passionate love for our brothers and sisters."

Will we not educate one another if we stay together as much as possible, breathing in, as it were, the same anxieties and suffering for the same ideals?

All educators look for and create such moments of real, constant, daily presence. What beautiful experiences we have had of community life during weeks when we lived together! What rich instruction our priests in youth ministry experienced in work camps or summer camping!

That is what the Lord desires of each of us: that we would be able to remain with him on our anxious journey when we are overly burdened with things and structures. O, to remain with Christ and know ourselves to be on the same wavelength with him; to slack our thirst from the same lifegiving water; to learn to will the same thing! "O to remain with you, Lord, and to draw our life from you and your sentiments, thoughts, and desires! Everything else would then come naturally: activity, devotion to undertakings, moving among the people."

"My dear disciple, you must not allow yourself to be seized by anxious desire that makes you want at all costs to do something for my kingdom. What matters to me is your breathing, your feeling, your thinking, the beating of your heart. It is there that my Spirit wants and looks for responses flowing from freedom. Above all, from your freedom as a disciple. It is there, too, that the great dialogue between my grace and your missionary activity takes place. In this dialogue my salvation is capable of capturing souls, conquering hearts that are uncertain, overcoming the barriers and difficulties that occur at any time. Too often—and on this point I must rebuke you as well, my dear disciple—people are anxious about what to do, and the result is that their activity is reduced to a jumble of under-takings, activity that attempts something new or activity that seeks to hold on to the old. A further result is that the apostolate loses its dynamism, its drawing power, its element of profound dialogue, its authenticity, authority, and credibility. It is in trials that disciples are judged. What is it that matters most to you: to overcome difficulties at any cost, or to keep your gaze first and foremost on me? If you keep your eyes on me, you will be able to find the right words at the right moment and the right thing to do. The more you keep your eyes on me, the more I will be able to teach you to love me in your brothers and sisters and to love them as no one else does—with my very heart."

"Yes, a disciple's proper dwelling place is your word, my God, and your gaze, O Christ! By your gaze scrutinize the depths of hearts and give insight, certitude, and a proper hierarchy among things."

There are so many suggestions I would like to make to you. There you have some of them; they are meant as guidelines, suggestions, stimuli.

Be Converted!

I have a clear sense that the command, Be converted!, is coming at us from many sides and that each of us, therefore, must be careful to hear that same command no less urgently within ourselves. We are living in the age of human rights, which people vehemently claim in mass protests. Individuals do not, however, seem equally convinced when it comes to their own habits, nor equally demanding when it comes to training themselves and others to live the rights thus acquired as obligations in conscience. People want to see structures and institutions transformed, but at the same time they hold to their narrow ways that are anchored in the past. When faced with certain harsh demands, I ask myself how reasonable people are or, better, to what extent they are really convinced in their wish for a more just world, since their own eye is still dull and their own heart so sick.

As for us of the household, is it really the Spirit who asks greater room for freedom or free dialogue, or is it at times, even frequently, simply a game we play of doing away with forms and plans, whereas in fact we are ready when the night has passed to arise the next morning the same persons as we were before? The Lord calls me to work for a kingdom in which each individual is personally called.

"You, my God, want my whole self, starting with a Yes that commits me soul and body."

"Yes, my dear disciple, it is precisely this that I ask of you: first listen to me, and then act. Reflect on my word and then proclaim it. I do not want you simply to be an instrument that utters sounds. After all, the created world adequately proclaims my wonderful deeds. Of you I ask freedom and life, consciousness and deep feelings. Thus and only thus will my word produce unexpected fruit in you."

"How marvelous your respect for me, Lord! How great and attractive my responsibility! Your call does not detract in any way from my personality; you want each of us to offer our gifts in the basket of our poverty."

The Interior Teacher

Of what use would all the words be if they did not open the heart to the voice deep within—almost imperceptible and unobtrusive—of this real divine presence? We must acknowledge that in our day [the Holy Spirit] is still the great unknown person of the Trinity; on the other hand, we seem to run the risk of speaking of him excessively and in cold abstractions that do not stir the soul of reader or hearer. That is my own great fear. And it is the reason why, instead of trying to talk about the Holy Spirit, I prefer to suggest that you consider living, concrete examples of what the Spirit has accomplished in the history of the Church. Why should we not rediscover, and update, the great spiritual tradition of Christianity? The Spirit is the heavenly Father's gift, and the gift of the dying and risen Christ. It is this Spirit who unveils the word of life for me in all its fullness. He lays hold of it and brings it, uncontaminated, down the centuries, and causes it to flower in the faith of each Christian.

"Speak to me, Spirit of God, and reveal all of Christ's secrets to me."

Letting the Spirit speak and express himself and be our counselor: is this not what happens in more intense prayer and when the soul's docility is complete? Fruits ripen in the seasons of the Spirit. Each season has its own sweet and flavorful fruits. And the Spirit has an infinite number of seasons. There are no limits, even of age. Let us learn to educate our little children and our young people for the unpredictable seasons of the Spirit! The human heart is always the same, yesterday and today: weak and unsure, full of doubts and bitterness. Sooner or later, in one way or another, people have need, indeed a great need, of a reliable message of comfort, a gaze from heaven.

"And you, my Christ, have instituted a sacrament of forgiveness and peace, life and joy. And the soul that kneels before you will be cheered by your touch."

It is said that the sacrament of Penance is passing through a crisis, precisely because the consciousness of ethical values is disappearing more and more. If nothing is sinful any more, why should I humble myself by kneeling in a confessional? But is it not the case that this moral crisis itself is due in part to the increasingly infrequent reception of the sacrament of God's forgiveness?

"My God, how can we come to understand the good, and therefore any omission or violation of it, if we do not dispose ourselves for the grace of God?"

"My kingdom is won daily, because the seed of goodness, justice, and freedom develops and produces its fruits. I instituted the sacrament of Penance as a school of humility and a way to become aware of the good that needs to be understood, loved, and struggled for. In your every weakness grace restores courage for your journey, and my kingdom shines out ever more brightly. I ask you to kneel frequently in confession, not only in order to heal your wounds, but also in order that you may discover more fully the wonders of my gospel and its power."

"My eyes look for your forgiveness, O Christ, and are more and more illumined by the attraction of your kingdom."

Among the many reasons why the confessional is deserted, one surely is an ignorance of the real value of this sacrament, along with our lack of openness to it and our lack of conviction when it comes to frequenting it regularly and educating the faithful to this sacramental expression of their faith.

"My God, how these gifts of yours—the Spirit and purifying grace—make us tremble with expectation, freighted as they are with everlasting hopes!"

Il Segno 6 (June 1990)

Chapter 7

Some truths may seem so obvious that only when we find ourselves having to talk about them in public do we realize what confusion exists in regard even to simple ideas. This has been my own experience at gatherings, discussions, and meetings. When, after explaining or thinking I had explained, fundamental aspects of church life, I have been met with questions or requests that show such uncertainties or such a fragmented faith that I ask myself whether we should not plead more often, and with tears, for the Spirit's gift of discernment. On the other hand, it is clear that prophetic insight is not a common possession and, in particular, that it is extremely difficult for everyone to live by clear principles and deep convictions. And yet there are clear ideas and principles of life: the light in the depths that no storm will ever succeed in extinguishing; the *joy of the gospel* which is felt even in darkness.

Sometimes, at some meetings, after having opened our hearts and spoken at length, do we not see the truth we have proclaimed running aground as it were amid the sands of problems that are seemingly vital but are in fact purely formal? People argue about parish, community, and youth ministry, movements and associations, deanery and overall pastoral plan. But where are the great themes of the Christian proclamation? Would not a few basic certainties, if authentically lived, suffice to resolve so many problems? And what is this certainty that helps harmonize missionary activity and ordinary pastoral practice, openness to the new and preservation of what we have—the parochial institution and movements, groups, and associations? Let us try to ask ourselves: What does tradition tell me? Let us go back for a moment to the origins, and let us ask ourselves: How did the Christian community arise? How was it established?

If we can answer the question "How is the Christian community structured?" we will be greatly helped in finding the right response to so many present-day pastoral problems and in putting these problems in their proper perspective. This is something which the contemporary mentality does not take for granted.

Apostolicity: The Foundation of Catholicity

I have already said it and I say it again: Mission activity preceded community and brought it into being. Historically, apostolicity is the foundation of catholicity. At the beginning there is always the gospel proclaimed, announced, and passed on from person to person, group to group. This is a disconcerting truth if we give it all the emphasis it deserves. First comes the word, then the structure. First the mission, then the formation of the community. Community is therefore founded on mission. The proclamation of the gospel goes before the disciples at every step and makes of them authentic missionaries, stimulating them never to let the journey weary them but to keep their contemplative gaze fixed on the paschal mystery. At the origin of everything there is, of course, a communion, that of the Trinity, but even this has "missions" within it.

Such is the living mirror into which every community, whether established or to be established, must look. The clouding of this mirror is a perennial source of difficulties. History has its lessons for us in this area.

Pastoral Practice—Ordinary and Missionary

While I view with great satisfaction the proliferation of praiseworthy initiatives in the diocese, I sometimes ask myself, Does all this have an interior or spiritual center from which the

41

impulses come? Is the option for the poor and crucified Jesus really at the heart of it all? If not, we are but a collection of new patches on an old garment!

See, people do one thing, but at the same do not want to neglect anything else. Some new proposal is made. It is immediately implemented. Is there an urgent need? Why not form a special committee? Delegation goes on and one thing is added to another. The resultant image is that of a lively, up-to-the-minute parish that heeds every voice in the wilderness. Let us honestly ask ourselves: Does this attentiveness really spring from the heart of a parish that judges by the purest proclamation of the gospel of Christ?

The issue is not to do more and more, nor to give preferential attention to one need rather than another. The real pastoral problem is simply to make a parish want the right thing, to instill in it a yearning for Christ. Then the rest will follow. And this rest will not mean the parish throwing itself into this or that field of work—pastoral care, for example, or catechesis—thus giving a privileged place to the least of the brothers and sisters or to those far off from the faith.

When one feels the beating of Christ's heart, every breath becomes his, no matter what the field in which one is working. Every parish activity is therefore loved and experienced and stamped with this mark of the gospel. Structures will also change and initiatives will flourish. What is already in place will remain, depending on its importance. And the new will make its appearance according to the measure of the freedom of the Spirit, who creates everything and re-creates it in Easter hope.

Sooner or later those who reflect on what I have been saying will be unable to refrain from asking, But then does the parish still have any meaning? What function can it have today? The same question arises at times, though less often than in the past, when I pursue the subject of missionary work. This is my answer: On the one hand, never so much as today has the need of the parish been felt—and this in all its forms, from the local level to the deanery level. At the same time, however, never so much as today do we want it to be more evangelical, that is, to be a believing community whose every breath is a loving one. This is a pastoral tension that is in constant need of harmonious resolution without depriving the local entity of its role in ordinary pastoral practice, and without holding back the irrepressible force of the missionary thrust. The missionary vocation is ordinarily lived out in parochial pastoral practice, while if ordinary pastoral practice is to be evangelical, it must draw upon the full missionary power of the gospel of Christ.

Toward a More Mission-minded Deanery

"Your Eminence, right now and very concretely, on what would you focus in order to restore greater vitality to the diocese of Milan?"

To tell the truth, I've never liked quick answers, especially when the problems are serious and important. At the same time, however, I did not feel that I could evade the question; as far as possible I had to avoid giving the impression, through a couple of proposals offered by way of example, that I was reducing the whole problem to a few strategies for action.

The diocese of Milan, due to its many problems and its heterogeneous situations and areas, requires a continuous process of collecting data, reading it, and interpreting it; and at the same time a contemplative gaze that constantly synthesizes all of this information. But on this occasion I risked a short answer, in more or less these words: "I would focus on two tasks: creating in each parish a well-nourished group of laypersons, and restoring the original missionary role of the deanery." Yes, I must repeat here, and everywhere the occasion offers, that it is indispensable to form convinced and consistent laypeople: mature Christians who are ready to work together and to bear witness in every environment. There is no valid excuse here: we must give time and energies to the development of this lay missionary consciousness in every parochial community. The pastoral council in these communities will be one important place for this development and cannot but become in its turn a spur to further growth. Associations such as Catholic Action have as their specific purpose the formation of such lay witnesses. If all believers make up the Church, why should they be marginalized? "It is difficult, Lord, to turn some convictions into a way of thinking and a community's life style!"

I would like to say a few words more on the importance of the deanery. It is important even if its geographical extent is small. I think I am not exaggerating when I say that the deanery contains the secret of a revival of faith throughout the diocese. How long shall we dig confidently in the field until we have discovered it? I have before me a little map of the diocese, and I see seventy-three deaneries clearly outlined. I would like to review the history of each. It is a lengthy history of faith: the solid faith of so many ordinary people, and a history of fidelity and sacrifice by the Lord's disciples.

"These deaneries are the same in number as the books of the Bible, Old and New Testaments. How can we help but be reminded of the seventy or seventy-two disciples who were your first missionaries, Lord? You sent them from town to town at your word."

We know that in the beginning Christianity found it easier to take root in urban centers, in order then to move out into surrounding rural areas, region after region, where the population was more scattered and inaccessible. The resulting group of parishes—urban and rural—in turn generated missionary activity in other urban centers, etc. The result was an irresistible spread outwards in concentric circles. In more recent times, what is to be said of these *groups of parishes* in which the foundational Church was regarded as vitally important? Today the name *group of parishes* has been replaced by the name *deanery*. Has only the name been changed? I wonder whether in addition to the name the old missionary role has also been lost. Is my wonder justified?

Let me say it forthrightly: a deanery is not to be regarded as simply an administrative and organizational structure, nor should its meetings be simply gatherings of colleagues in order to exchange views or experiences and to organize some joint activities. A deanery is indeed that, but it should not be only that. It is absolutely necessary to restore the deanery's life-giving soul.

Admittedly, we must first be convinced with all our souls that we are in the same position as the first Christian communities, which did not remain isolated or closed in on themselves in order to enjoy their little world as believers in Christ. Rather than being an expression of the life of the various parishes that constitute it, a deanery must increasingly become a vital, dynamic center in order to enrich the faith of poor parishes, support the weak ones, and revitalize those that are worn out—all in a truly apostolic spirit and with the very love of Christ himself. The pastoral council of the deanery must not simply be a set of representatives of the various communities but must become instead a source of strength with a missionary responsibility. And it must always have a profoundly evangelical spirit.

"The need is not to judge, Lord, but to know that we are brothers and sisters together, in your name!"

At times I hear complaints about the absence of various parishes from the life of the deanery: "It's because they are jealous, or afraid that others will come in and invade their territory . . ." If it were simply a matter of jealousy, I would not be greatly worried. Even jealousy may have its positive side, for it can be a sign of great attachment to one's own little garden, which one cultivates dutifully and at the cost of great daily sacrifice. Would that there were some discussion of the isolation which people cultivate out of fear that unity might take something away from them! But when we keep something good for ourselves, do we not commit a sin of omission against those who need it? The riches of faith must be given away. Otherwise faith becomes sterile and loses its savor even for one's own community.

But the thing I wonder about is different: there is an unwillingness to give credit to the deanery for fear of change—not living any longer on a private income, as it were, or losing traditions that are now at death's door. Are people perhaps already resigned to simply surviving as long as possible, without too much bother?

"*That*, Lord, frightens me!"

Il Segno 7–8 (July–August 1990)

Chapter 8

I was on my way home and still feeling entangled in all the questions and doubts, all the strong desires for clarification and more convincing arguments. The discussion concerned the usual dilemma: How are we to win the people of our day? How are we to dialogue with them? Are we to be more lenient or are we to hold fast to principles and traditions? I listened with lively interest, as always, trying to sense the good faith of each of the speakers and their impassioned arguments.

Martyrdom and Dialogue

In the accumulation of pros and cons, I felt that people were both trying to win me to their side and passing judgment on me—some leniently, others rigidly. Was not my chief strength (I told myself) my ability to understand my brothers and sisters? I had to give an answer, but an answer which allowed room for dialogue and did not close the door on further inquiry:

> Never so strongly as today, brothers and sisters, have people felt the urgent need of sincere dialogue and of building bridges between all, yet, at the same time, felt such fears and perplexities. From the beginning the Lord wanted dialogue with people. He offered such dialogue in countless forms. Was not the covenant the most extraordinary of these forms? The first great covenant put the fidelity of the people to a hard test, while even the final covenant continues to test rigorously the fidelity of the

entire human race. I would like to tell you now one of my own deepest convictions. The whole question of confrontation versus dialogue with today's world should not be reduced to a practical choice of pastoral methods: openness or rigidity, smiles or rebukes, extending a hand to everyone or keeping ourselves as much on guard as possible. The real issue is fidelity to Christ and his saving word. The real issue is faith—faith in the divine covenant.

I wanted to continue but I found myself cut off, as it were. I seemed to be saying things that required no discussion, to be offering the usual remarks about the God who loves us and about our duty of obeying him. At the same time, I realized the existential difficulties involved in proclaiming the gospel to a complex society that is no different in many of its attitudes from the society of the Old Testament. I was living once again the tragic fate of Moses: absolute fidelity to the God of the covenant and a strong attachment to his own people. As I reflected on these matters during my return journey, after that lively exchange of opinions, my own soul also looked for an answer. An answer better than my poor words.

"My God, speak to us anew, and let your word lift up our spirits."

"My dear disciples, I feel your piercing gaze and the agitation in the hearts of so many pastors. You ask me for a sure answer, and I ask you a question in return: What is it today that most bewilders this world and keeps it far from me? The great inconsistencies of Christians or their lack of faith in me?"

Some want to reply immediately and point the finger at the great inconsistencies. But silence prevails, as the answer is awaited: the answer of God.

"It is the lack of faith in my word that leads to uncertainties and infidelity. The inconsistencies certainly do cause conflicts of conscience and no little confusion. But is the lack of faith in my love any less provoking? What sense does it make to claim to save the world, while you live in an enclave within this world that needs also to be saved? Prophetic souls are needed who look ahead with a lively and penetrating gaze. You still think of my martyrs as people who perform a great action at the end of their lives, people who are admired and glorified but who do not help with your everyday problem of pastoral 'method.' Martyrdom, you say, is something extraordinary that does not teach us how daily to lead to God those who are far off from him. What we need now is new pastoral methods! you say. But is it really true that martyrdom does not teach us a pastoral method? Is it really true that the martyr's willingness to lose everything in order to safeguard faith and conscience is not in fact at the heart of every problem, even the problem of a pastoral approach to those who are distant?"

"Lord, your words make us think. Martyrdom is the 'simplest' thing there is because it focuses exclusively on what is essential. But we are afraid of the essential, that is, of a limitless faith in your word, and we gamble with it every moment of our lives, since it is this essential alone that transforms everything else. What is martyrdom but the purest and most authentic proof of fidelity to you, Lord, and to your children?"

The greater our faith in God, the more we will give ourselves to our brothers and sisters with a purer and more persuasive love. *That* is the dialogue proper to the kingdom of God. Furthermore, every authentic gift is always a form of martyrdom: a dying in order to give life—like the seed that dies and then becomes an ear of grain bursting with life. Every vocation is a renunciation for the sake of hope, like the day which comes to an end in order to bring about a new dawn. To dialogue with the world is to love it in God and to give everything—energies, time, and life itself, if need be—to the brothers and sisters. The most profound dialogue is the dialogue of faith and not of our human words. To dialogue is to contemplate God while carrying all that is human in our hearts.

"Lord, what do your martyrs who shed their blood have to say to our world? That everything is finished? That there is no hope left? That dialogue is impossible? No, they say—and this is their testimony—that you are the God of the living and that eternal life is here, today, in the blood they have given, for this blood is the seed of hope in love eternal. Is not the most credible testimony to your dialogue with the world the cross of Jesus, where a new covenant is made in the blood of a universal and unending gift? Are not these two extended arms a cosmic embrace that will last until the end of the world?"

Dialogue and Proselytism

The power of martyrdom, the readiness to give our life for our faith and for those we love, is the root of all missionary preaching. There is no contradiction between preaching and dialogue when the dialogue is supported by the interior power that makes us put our lives on the line for the word of God and the welfare of our brothers and sisters. Quite different is the attitude and approach to others which we call proselytism. The word *proselytism* does not have a negative connotation in and of itself. In the Bible proselytes were those people from the pagan world who were "drawing near" (that is the original meaning of the word) to the God of the Hebrews. Even at that time, however, the word could indeed suggest a drawing near that was not spontaneous but to some extent coerced by pressures that did not respect the interior journey of the individual. This negative connotation is evident, for example, in the words of Jesus: "Woe to you who cross sea and land to make a single proselyte; having gotten him, you make him twice as much a child of hell as yourselves" (Matt 23:15). We might paraphrase and say that proselytism in the negative sense consists in an approach to the other which is motivated solely by a desire "to make him one of us." In the foreground is not the word of God and the love of Christ but the desire to increase the power of the group. Proselytism, thus understood, betrays a lust for power that is satisfied by increasing the number of followers. This observation applies not only to religious proselytism but to proselytism practiced by any group, be it social, political, cultural, athletic, or any other.

The boundary between authentic proclamation and proselytism of a negative kind is not always easy to draw. But people today are especially sensitive to the difference. True proclamation has its root in martyrdom, that is, in the readiness to give our life out of love. It demands, above all else, that we desire to be like Jesus and with Jesus, to stand at his side, to imitate him and work with him. This kind of life (which is a manner of "being") gives rise to many-sided and authentically missionary action. Such missionary action will operate chiefly by radiation or contagion. The point of such metaphorical language is that, just as the sun radiates light and heat not because of something added to its essential self but by the very fact of its being the sun, and as certain positive or negative qualities infect others not by some special action but because they are by nature suited to spread themselves, so too true love of Jesus is a light and power that radiates to others simply because it exists and exists in abundance. This is the basic missionary activity proper to every Christian, young or old, rich or poor, influential or unimportant, healthy or sick. It is not a missionary activity that requires something further, because it is inherent in the radiating power of the gospel when the gospel is truly lived. Consequently, when we worry so much about the "missionary character" of our communities, we would do well to ask whether or not these communities take seriously the living of the gospel.

There is also an explicit missionary activity that takes the form of proclamation or preaching, that is, giving reason for our hope, expressing this hope with conviction and simplicity, and offering it as a treasure to which we want all to have access. This kind of missionary activity presupposes the first kind, the mission of "radiation," and continues and completes it. The second kind of activity occurs especially in two circumstances: dispersion and mandate. We have the first when one or more Christians, who have no special missionary intention, find themselves outside their usual place or their own community and begin to radiate the gospel and talk about it. We have the second when a specific plan of evangelization is implemented.

The Acts of the Apostles gives examples of these different kinds of missionary activity. In the early chapters of Acts we see a community that is acquiring its internal organization and seems unconcerned with any mission outside Jerusalem. But "crowds rushed in to Jerusalem from neighboring towns" (Acts 5:16). This is an instance of radiation. In chapter 8 there is a scattering of Christians caused by the persecution of Stephen, with a resulting radiation and proclamation to peoples and places no one had originally had in mind. Chapter 13 tells of a specific plan of evangelization, and it involves a mandate given to Barnabas and Paul.

The emphasis today on the institutional side of the Church brings with it the danger of understanding mission as *Churching:* you, too, must become one of us. But mission means first and foremost the radiating of Jesus, his grace, his risen life, his salvation. "The Lord was daily adding to the community those who were being saved" (Acts 2:47). It is the Lord who calls; it is he who is the focus of mission; it is he who gives salvation. The community's role is to receive with love those whom the Lord has called and who have answered the call.

Il Segno 9 (September 1990)

Chapter 9

At the same meeting I referred to in the last chapter, I found myself many times on the point of spontaneously interrupting to rebut various questions and to urge the questioners to reread the preceding pastoral programs more attentively.

Eucharist as Summit

I wondered deeply (as I had in *Attirerò tutti a me [I Will Draw All to Myself]*) whether the documents of the Church, including the local Church, "keep their bloom for us for only a few months and then are forgotten without producing solid results." At the end of that intense and humanly disturbing day, my soul felt weighed down and it sought illumination. Answers from God seemed slow in coming, downcast as I was at the thought of having to deal with so many whys and wherefores that followed after so many failures to understand and to follow through on previous pastoral plans. I asked myself frankly: do we Christians really believe with all our souls in the great proclamation of our faith?

"But you, O Christ, are the only Savior, and only through direct encounter with you can any human being find salvation! Why, then, do we wrestle with paltry matters and not allow ourselves to be dazzled by your saving love?"

One question in particular had disturbed me in my silence: how can we bring this mystery closer to our people? This question brought to mind what I had written in *Attirerò tutti a me*, pages which I had carefully thought out with deep feeling. I thought to myself that the questioner could have found in them the answers to his many questions as well as powerful encouragement in overcoming his fears.

A priest well on in years once told me: "I celebrate Mass every day in a poor, tiny church, with a few people present. And yet, don't ask me why, but I feel as if the entire world were close at hand. The silence within the four walls becomes the voice of all those absent, and I feel Christ alive in my hands there as in no other place." Yes, it is not the faithful, be they many or few, who make the Mass, but the Mass turns all, present or absent, into people "saved" in Christ. Christ, the God-human, who is a constant dialogue, willed the Church, and wills it still, to be the great sacrament of salvation. And the Church is this great sacrament because it proclaims, celebrates, and lives the mystery of Christ, the Savior of the world.

The Eucharist is the greatest proclamation, the greatest celebration of this mystery that embraces human beings, each and all of them, and gives them back the freedom to live. When we celebrate the sacrifice of Christ, how can we fail to think of ourselves as being first of all his ministers: involved and drawn by the mystery, and educated to love the Son of God above all else?

"Lord Jesus, your mystery is here in our hands, and our hands are cold!"

From Eucharist to Freedom

The Lord's voice within me now spoke clearly, and I had great need of it. I felt a thirst not so much for words as for grace, the grace which Christ had given me in abundance at my sacramental ordination and which finds ritual expression in every Eucharist I celebrate: "My disciple, your mission is an important one. I chose you for great things: to be my collaborator in the salvation of humanity through its deliverance from slavery to evil. The world neither asks nor expects anything other than this: my freedom. *My* freedom because freedom is my prerogative alone. The freedom of human beings is, again, *my* freedom, because I created them and paid a heavy price for my love of them, and I want them to be saved."

"Human freedom: how spoiled the word has become, and how scorned the reality! But your freedom, Lord, is here, within me, ready to give me new life and to make me in turn a liberator of captive freedom."

Our calling is a great one, and no less great is our responsibility. Christ does not call us to petty chores within the house, but rather to restore to this house its divinely intended immensity, in which every creature may feel itself to be truly a son or daughter and a brother or sister. Our important mission is to say to the people we see: "do not let yourselves be lost in the fog of your illusions! Seek the nobility God wants for you! *That* is your dignity!" And our mission is to say to our brothers and sisters who are far off: "God has not forgotten you! But seek him with all your heart!"

Christ calls us to make alive in the heart of each of our brothers and sisters that longing for the infinite, or that emptiness of pure freedom, that gives the right rhythm to their steps toward the absolute Good. Our mission is to keep alive and alert the hope of a better tomorrow. This is no small thing in a world in which an acclaimed and accelerated progress is accompanied by prospects of an inevitable decline with awful fears of planetary self-destruction. Decline and destruction are not the meaning of the cross of Christ.

"The light of a hope filled with promise already bathes your cross, O Christ, as you surrender to the Father and as I am spent by persevering faithfully."

In every decline, Christ is here to break his bread for us once again and to hearten his disciples, his sons and daughters, who are scattered to every corner of the earth. At the breaking of the bread on the evening of the first Easter the two disciples open their hearts to a new hope and return joyfully to Jerusalem. At the breaking of the bread we too should feel drawn by the mystery and should proclaim it.

"How can we bring this mystery closer to our people?"

Here, now, is the answer: It is the Eucharist that must shape every believing community and renew the world. Christ's Passover, celebrated and mysteriously set before us and revisited in the Eucharist, contains all the power to draw the world. Here is my and your apostolic mission in all its fullness.

"Here, O Christ, in your suffering, death, and resurrection, everything is contained: the Father's boundless love, your own sacrifice and unqualified obedience, and the gift of your Spirit's freedom."

"It is your freedom that I love," says the Lord, "and on this freedom everything depends: your own tomorrow and the tomorrow of all humankind. You cannot take wild risks and run after wild fancies. Trust in me once and for all, and the evil one will stop throttling your will. O you of little faith, you have not yet reached the dusk; a new light is rising. Do you not see how secular ideologies are in decline?"

Let us not lose this great opportunity for restoring to a disillusioned humanity the nostalgia for God and the thirst for life-giving freedom. Let us renew the way of life to which faithful disciples of Christ are called. Let us leave our fears behind, shake off all formality and narrow-mindedness, and recover the courage of the first missionaries of the gospel. Great faith is needed in more difficult and demanding situations. Divine certainties are needed after age-old illusions and the collapse of ideals. People must begin once again to trust in God and in his word that does not deceive. Only in this way will they win back the freedom they have betrayed and once again have confidence in themselves.

As for us, disciples of the true bread that is to be broken in every human heart, are we witnesses to this new world of freedom? If every Mass produced in me a glimmer of a more convinced faith and if the mystery of Christ took on greater solidity for me, would we not have more flourishing communities, communities on the missionary journey?

Concern for Human Freedom

This evening at dusk, as I looked out to sea, my spirit desired to remain concentrated for as long as possible on the reality of God, the giver of freedom. At the same time, I could not but think of the long human journey down the centuries toward a fuller awareness of personal individuality and freedom. However (I thought), it is not from historical humanity that I ought to start in trying to understand something of this blessed freedom. The human struggle convinces me of the importance of freedom, but it does not reveal the secret of freedom. I need to focus my gaze wholly on God and question him as fully as possible so that I may obtain at least some moment of illumination and then allow this to make an impression on me interiorly. If I cling to my limitations, I shall never be able to understand why I thirst for freedom and where I am to quench this thirst.

In *Attirerò tutti a me* I wrote: "Freedom is not its own end but finds this end by trusting."

"Did you really believe this? Do you still? Do you, a human being who longs for the purer air of freedom, know that you risk bitter disappointments if you do not lift your eyes to the heights? You must open yourself to the mystery of God. There is no other path. Otherwise you will have run in vain, through an endless wilderness. You must entrust yourself to Christ, for he alone possesses the secret of your freedom and mine, and you must not be afraid of Christ. He does not rob you of any of your deepest yearnings for life. Rather he purifies them and enobles them with an unimaginable greatness."

"Yet here we are, Lord, still deceiving ourselves with meager human crumbs and stubbornly thinking up ideals for living, secular utopias, and messianic promises."

And you, who are a committed Christian, or a religious man or woman, or a priest, do you not grasp the seriousness of your mission? Do you not feel its attraction? See, Christ gives you the power to set human beings free, *any* human being, whatever his or her slavery. To such a brother or sister you can say without fear:

> You are free, if you wish to be free! Trust in the message that saves! In Christ you will discover the ability to choose the good, to base your judgments on it in the complexities of social life, and to study it in depth in moments of uncertainty. Grace does

not by any means mortify your sincere quest of the paths of freedom, but is always ready to bring light into your thoughts and expectations, to forgive your uncertainties, and to give new vigor to your hopes.

We cannot restrict ourselves, dear colleagues, to gathering proposals and listening to voices calling for help: this is one step, but we must go further. Human beings seek freedom, hunger for it, and want it at any cost, and I as a disciple of Christ cannot give vague answers. I must tell them: Christ alone can broaden and deepen your longing and make your dream come true.

"Have faith, and be courageous!"

At this point, my meditation that evening made its sting felt. How could I fail to suffer at the quenching of vigorous souls and the death of profound expectations? Why on earth is it that the more abundance and prosperity the human spirit achieves, the more it seems to slacken in its longing for God and its concern for the brothers and sisters? The impression we have is that a smooth sea and easy sailing lull sailors. On a troubled sea each sailor is busy struggling to keep alive.

But the Lord made his presence felt in my prayer: "You, my disciple, must not be afraid to face up to present-day reality as it is. You must prod it with my grace. Then you yourself will continue to be prodded by it in faith. There are expectations that are still alive and expectations already quenched. There are desires that spur people on, and desires the edges of which are now blunted. There are convictions that are still stubborn and convictions that are worn out. You must, on the one hand, provide certainties and, on the other, arouse hope. Because you are a man who is called, you will emerge from the clash with this reality as one strengthened in faith and hope; you will mature more quickly, become more expert in the art of persuasive dialogue, and rediscover its values, its capacities for the divine. The more you struggle, the more you will realize the power of my lifegiving word. My freedom is able to dissolve every lump of evil. Have faith, be courageous!"

Il Segno 10 (October 1990)

Chapter 10

I feel a deep need, as a believer, to contemplate tirelessly this marvelous Church of mine, this inexhaustible spring of life-giving waters.

"Yes, you are a mystery of never-ending grace, and my spirit is drawn by your power to set people free. In you, moreover, beloved Church of Christ, every human weakness sooner or later melts away under the breath of this Spirit of freedom who causes the divine gaze to rest on hopes and expectations that are never quenched. Father, I praise you! Son of love, I thank you! In you is my hope, O Spirit of freedom!"

There is but one kingdom, that of Christ, in which God's gifts become seeds of promise in the hearts of each person and grace flows uninterruptedly like beneficent rain to make these seeds grow and reach maturity. This kingdom fascinates me with its potentiality for life and its irresistible advance toward the true freedom of the individual and the human race. Christ's freedom is present here in the heart of this Church which no power can halt. And in the heart of this great Church my own heart beats as does the heart of every disciple of Christ and the faith of every community.

I see promising communities, and the flowering of vocations that are open to the newness of the gospel and are guided by the Spirit. Such is the richness of the Church of Christ, which draws and gives itself, stirs deeply felt needs, and becomes a saving response on behalf of all. "Lord, what gifts of love your Church possesses!" I see laypeople increasingly taking up the journey, conscious of their ability to be an authoritative voice of the Church. The masses are emerging from centuries of anonymity; they are looking for a visage of their own, an identity, a responsibility.

"This kingdom of yours, O Christ, calls all to freedom, and the way of freedom is the way of responsibility."

We must not be afraid because the laity are becoming ever more conscious of their identity in the Church of Christ. Their identity is their dignity as sons and daughters and their responsibility for the kingdom. Any community that is authentically missionary has the urgent task of maturing the laity to this end. The Church of Christ loves the freedom of its children. The freer persons are in Christ, the more they feel responsible for the kingdom. We who are disciples of Christ are called to quicken the freedom of each individual for the sake of their own growth and the growth of the entire kingdom. Contemporary society feels the urgent need of such freedom, and so ought we, the ministers of the Christ who wills that all become free and be saved.

You Christian laymen and laywomen who are listening to me: you feel the attraction of this Church and you want to be living parts of it, with head and heart, with hands that endure fatigue and bear witness that everything has been redeemed by the cross of Christ. You sense the mystery of Christ's freedom and you would like to bear witness to it with the power of your faith and the faith of your community. You would like to, but you do not always do it. Sometimes you feel isolated, even dead. Remember: today the Church relies on you, and I too rely on you, in order that this Church of ours in the diocese of Milan may prosper again on the path of freedom; for, though all desire it, this path is made difficult by an anonymous and indifferent mass of people and the great timidity of the disciples of Christ.

"These faithful laypeople of yours, Lord, desire to be the Church, to be missionary voices and give missionary witness."

Great especially is the responsibility of Christian spouses. Their call to the sacrament of matrimony gives joy to all and is an example for all, a testimony to faith and to the love that turns itself into a home open to all. A Christian community will feel more of the missionary spirit in the measure that the family is able to recover its prophetic role: as a united family, as the foundation of society, as parents who form their children for a better tomorrow, as a cell of faith that has the ability to vitalize parish life and open it to the goodness and generosity of the Father. The Christian family is the great saving sacrament for a society that is undergoing a major crisis of values.

"Lord, set our human hearts free and give them the freedom to live an authentic life. Your sacrament will then consecrate new families, prophetic families, missionary families."

All are not called to live the same vocation in this wonderful kingdom of Christ. God's generosity is magnificent and its ways cannot be anticipated; it is always creative. The rays that emanate from the gaze of God are many. There are also calls to a special consecration, and the forms they take are both old and new. These calls are invaluable sources of illumination, living testimonies that the freedom of Christ is at work in our deepest selves and that love is the purest form of the gift of life in the service of the brothers and sisters. These vocations insistently remind us that the absolute good demands first place and that divine providence is at work amid the poverty of our means and the things from which we benefit. These vocations are a source of great hope for tomorrow's world, hope which the structures that presently burden us may keep from swift fulfillment but will never extinguish.

"These special calls of yours, O Lord, are the richest gifts of your freedom. And you know how much we need them!"

We must educate the young to make this kind of choice, and we must be courageous in proposing such a choice. The more we set them free in their education, the more they will be attracted by religious vocations. Today's young people do not like half-measures. The experiences of recent years (Shechem Assembly, Samuel Group) have shown that in today's young men and women are to be found vast and unexplored vocational potentialities.

We must also make the most of and carefully assess vocations to the permanent diaconate. This is a new form of evangelization, and these deacons certainly can in the near future fulfill a pastoral role both at the heart of the diocese and on a broader scale, especially in the areas of service and catechetics. In a kingdom that is increasingly open to the saving grace of Christ through new and bold responses, the role of the presbyter also needs clarification and a fuller understanding. "Every call, Lord, is from you, and you issue your calls at every moment. Today your kingdom requires humble service, full self-giving, and great obedience even to your local Church."

The urgency of today's mission raises serious questions about our apostolate and compels us to listen to the voice of God once more without setting restrictions on it and then to grasp the mystery of his call. God has called us and continues calling us to proclaim the good news in a society that is reaching the end of the second millennium. And "society" includes the entire complex of human realities in which we can see at every moment how difficult it is to remain pure of heart and believers in the invisible, how urgent it is to be humble instruments of a mystery that never fails: the mystery of a Christ who does not allow a single apostolic breath we draw to fall into a void, even for a moment.

"This *today*, like all others, is yours, Lord. Why then should we be afraid of it? And you call me to inspire greater freedom in facing it."

Our vocation, dear colleagues, is to proclaim the gospel *today* and to say to *this* concrete brother or sister, "Today you can be saved and live by the liberating grace of Christ." We cannot shift on to others that which is our own specific task, nor can we ourselves take on useless tasks or tasks which others can and should carry out. Our mission is to devote an intense faith and life to evangelization, focusing on the essentials of the gospel, including the educating of souls in the essentials of freedom.

"Too many occupations weigh down the spirit, and, Lord, how your community suffers from this!"

In a parish the priest is the center, the person who stirs latent energies and prophetic spirits, and coordinates them as parts of a common effort to give Christian inspiration to the community and to carry on a dialogue with those who are far off. The parish certainly has its irreplaceable function, but so does the deanery and the diocese as a whole. It is for the bishop to make use of his priests, some for more specific tasks, others for more general responsibilities. The bishop must inspire his diocese to serve the Lord through the application of all its forces, which may be humble but are used in a spirited way, and through the readiness of his priests to undertake missions that are not always easy. For this reason every priest is a missionary, even in his parish. This means he is ready for every call. In this matter we in Milan need perhaps a greater freedom of spirit, so as not to let the parameters be set for us by entrenched structures and situations that tend to place us, too, "beyond removal."

"Lord, we are not officials, we are your servants! Give us the strength to look upon ourselves as useless servants and yet always be ready to repeat our Yes!"

Institutional Renewal

The institution will also be constantly renewed along with the renewal of the community of believers, provided the Christian laity and the priests and those consecrated to Christ become more receptive to the creative breath of the Spirit. When we speak of institutions we are referring first of all to the diocese and, in our case, to its great size. Our diocese has often been called the largest diocese in the world (and to some extent this is true). "How can all of us, Lord, not feel the burden of its size?" But I also see and feel its nobler energies at work, as well as the shock of its needs and anxieties. I continually ask for the grace to be able to listen very attentively to this whole world of demands and expectations. "As for you, O Lord, do you not call whom you will and as you will? And at every moment?"

The diocese places its trust in all the workers of the first hour and it places its hope in those of the last hour. This kingdom of Christ must heed every prophetic voice, assess every new demand, and distinguish between hope inspired by Christ and a momentary longing. What I am asking now of every colleague I also ask of the entire faith community and the members of Church groups or associations or movements. The diocese needs all of us. Every fervent and spirited suggestion should be a stimulus to it. Such is our obligation. The kingdom of Christ, too, requires this. But the diocese also asks each of us for collaboration, dialogue, and the facing of problems—with explicit reference to the local bishop and to diocesan plans with the great undertakings to which all are asked to contribute.

A diocese grows and matures in the measure that its sons and daughters, its communities, and its groups or movements grow and mature. And where does it grow and mature? In the kingdom of God, [working through] structures that can be renewed though not easily replaced. They should not be renewed by moving or knocking down existing structures and risking replacing them with others that are more narrowing and burdensome. It is human beings that need to be refashioned, according to the measure of the freedom of Christ. And they are ordinarily renewed by leaving them in their workplace and living environment, provided they now work and live as redeemed sons and daughters.

Missionary Parishes

At this point I would like to speak, though briefly, of the parish as social setting, as the place which—like it or not—is a world for each individual, as a faith-inspired structure which despite all its limitations and deficiencies is still a source of strong cohesiveness. It is the missionary spirit of the parish that needs to be reassessed. Here lies the secret of renewal of the parish: the rediscovery of its innate missionary thrust. I have already written several times on this subject, and I think it is my duty to take it up again, especially since I fear it has not yet been completely understood by all.

How is it possible to ensure that a parish will have this great missionary spirit? Perhaps by removing its geographical boundaries? Or by removing its territorial character and, consequently, its relation to the families, children, lonely elderly people, and sick who live in this territory? The need, rather, is to broaden the patterns of thinking that bind people in too restricted a way. A community progresses when it believes in the mission of Christ, who tells it: "Be consistent when you go to the workplace! Do not close your eyes to human misery! Seek justice for the poor!" Then individuals will feel themselves to be missionaries, but with their base in the parish community which gives them strength, stimulus, incentive, support, and hope in undertaking their mission, within the parish or elsewhere. Membership in a group or movement should lead persons to respect and love their parish and to work collaboratively for this kingdom of God which makes me feel, no matter where I go, that I am a son or daughter, a brother or sister to all and that I journey together with the poorer and less endowed.

Missionary Attitudes

Talk of the essentials—of poverty, self-giving, and brotherhood or sisterhood—may seem perfectly obvious given the extent to which these attitudes, which give activity its true gospel style, are verbally accepted by ecclesiastical public opinion and recalled in retreats and all kinds of meetings for prayer and reflection. Almost no one among us calls them into doubt at the theoretical level. "But do we seriously believe, Lord, that if we do not put them fully into practice we are still far from your kingdom?" I am tempted to illustrate these unchallenged attitudes from the concrete testimony of saints ancient or modern, or of great laypersons or priests who have lived among us. I might remind the reader of Blessed Pier Giorgio Frassati, of Marcello Candia, or of Don Luigi Monza. But I do not want to give the impression that when all is said and done the full living of such an apostolic way of life is for only a few, that we are dealing here with exceptional cases, privileged lives that arouse admiration but nothing more.

Poverty, selfless giving, and brotherhood and sisterhood are the traits common to the sanctity to which we are all called in the Church of Christ. The reign of God obliges us to live the evangelical life style. God's is a kingdom that calls for a daily witness of poverty and self-giving, focus on the essentials, and brotherhood and sisterhood. The word of truth and love is inseparable from attitudes that make us transparent to God and our brothers and sisters and render us full of confidence in God alone and therefore at the service of the whole world. The word of God also becomes flesh in these attitudes and speaks through them without words.

I find it hard to talk about the authentic style of a disciple and a Christian because none of us escapes conventional thought patterns and trite words. Then, too, words persuade only to a certain point. They pass quickly, and everyday life is always there to tell me: Ideas are beautiful and ideals wonderful . . . but you do what you can! "O God, is that really our manner of life?"

Our apostolate is in danger of becoming a swollen mass of things, of succumbing to fads that disappear at the first shadows. It is essential that we focus on educational values, which are to be advanced with all our energies; I mean the values of the kingdom which bestow dignity and conscientiousness, responsibility and hope on human beings. And what of the encounter of two freedoms—that of Christ which sets free, and our human insufficiency—which establish the proper hierarchy in my apostolate? "Think of how we overdo it, Lord; yet after all that sweat what have I left?" Yet we disciples of Christ know well what the kingdom of God is. We teach it to everyone, children and adults. And we talk loudly about the primacy of the spirit that is to be saved. And then? "We get lost in countless rivulets of activity that dissipate the freshness of your wellspring, O God of love."

Then there is poverty, another characteristic attitude in the missionary style. It is an attitude that reveals more than anything else whether we are truly free in soul; that is, whether we really believe in the word that liberates and saves or whether, on the other hand, we set alongside the word we preach count-less shadows or surrogates, in the name, of course, of necessity or demands which in the end only constrict the soul and make it harder for it to breathe the air of the mystery. We believe in God but at the same time we do not manage to detach our-selves from possessions that are troublesome or hold us back on the journey of faith. How can your freedom, O Christ, put up with our possessions, which are so many useless paltry ob-sessions or silly ways of obtaining security?

The whole character of the kingdom of God is conveyed in that beautiful passage in Matthew 5:25-34. God knows how much we need to meditate on it at length and to base our man-ner of apostolate on it. We rely too much on human measures and then let ourselves be tied down in hand and heart by too many compromises. Structures and environments are neces-sary, but let us not weary of making sure they have a real soul. It is the presence of magnanimous educators that guarantees these structures and makes them sound. The hearts of our people, from the youngest to the oldest, should find here, in our parochial structures, further reason for struggling for a bet-ter world, and the educational desire which elsewhere has trouble making itself heard, so heavy is the air people breathe there. "We are richly endowed with a freedom that gives hope even to the dead, and yet we persist, Lord, in wanting to save this world by ourselves multiplying five loaves and two fishes."

When our hearts are free of superfluous burdens and we breathe the air of Christ's freedom, then our brothers and sis-ters too will experience the intoxication of the Spirit of life and our communities will feel less tied down by soulless struc-tures. It is here that the giving of self without expectation of re-ward comes in, the attitude of living in the light of God's liberality rather than that of human precautions. This self-giving makes the missionary way of life truly credible in its activities. It is this that frees me from the danger of profession-alism. It places me at the service of Christ's freedom as I share the journey of the neediest among my brothers and sisters, those who are unable to repay me or even to thank me.

Priority belongs to self-giving, which makes me rely not on any human satisfaction. It allows me to sow without waiting for any buds to appear, to labor in a kingdom in which the only certainty is that Christ is mysteriously present. "This is the essence of self-surrender, Lord: to give myself without self-interest, in the service of the human heart."

Finally, there is brotherhood and sisterhood. The entire Christian life-style can be summed up as a brotherhood and sisterhood that acknowledges no limits. Those who live by the essentials and in poverty and self-giving will sooner or later succeed in sincere dialogue with all. Those who are able to surrender everything for love of Christ have no concern except for their brothers and sisters.

I greatly desire that all would understand how important it is to believe with all our hearts in the freedom of Christ and to make this our life-style, if we want to hear, understand, and enter into dialogue with today's world. And this hearing, understanding and communication come into being within my own setting and my daily relationships. A community that lives the missionary life-style is a community of brothers and sisters who are serious about loving one another and are ready for dialogue with those near and far. Here is where the way for the Church and for human freedom is to be found: in the freedom of Christ to which fervent disciples and communities know how to bear witness in evangelical fashion.

The message of Christ requires precisely these things of us: focus on the essentials, poverty, free self-giving, and brotherhood and sisterhood. "Everything else will be added, Lord, if you will it."

Il Segno 11 (November 1990)

Chapter 11

We may paraphrase St. Augustine and say of our time: "The heart of the Church will be restless until the whole world finds rest in the peace of Christ." Jesus made his command clear: "Go, therefore, and teach all nations," and this command determines the very nature of the Catholic Church which regards itself as pressed by love of Christ to become a missionary to all peoples.

I have the impression at times that people think they should *also* be interested in the missions, and in saying this I do not mean to detract in any way from their praiseworthy activities in this area. But the Church is not *also* missionary: it *is* missionary, because and to the extent that it is the Church of Christ. It is not so much a matter of the Church *commanding*, as of the Church itself *being commanded* by the risen Christ. "Your Church, O Christ, is always in a state of mission." In its entirety and everywhere. In our day we may not consider the young Churches in the missions to be unimportant.

The Church is constantly in a state of mission. And, in a life-giving interplay of grace and faith, this mission quickens and is quickened by fresh energies that come from afar and invite us to an ever new journey. To those who complain about being overly committed in the parishes so that they are completely absorbed and have no time for anything outside their own little garden, this must be said: "A time is coming when new blood will have to be put in the now blocked veins of certain structures. Peoples presently forgotten or mistreated and so-called primitive civilizations represent springtime on the way. They will enable our exhausted Western civilization to emerge from its winter torpor, if it has the wisdom to accept them."

The more the Church evangelizes and expands its boundaries, the more it will be renewed and the more it will become aware of itself, recover its vigor, and be enriched by priceless values that have been hidden for centuries in forests or mistreated areas of our European civilization. How many opportunites have been lost due to pride of race or culture or faith! How many fields there are that are boundless in expanse and contain treasures still undiscovered! And yet here we stubborn folk remain, supposedly enjoying fruits now past their prime! We need gusts of fresh air, we need smiles that are a little less routine. Even our parishes will bloom again!

A parish priest from a little village said to me: "There are such great opportunities today for linking the parishes with the Churches in the mission countries. I myself am very fortunate to have a community rich in missionary vocations. And I try to keep alive our links with them. The people here ought to feel involved with these missionaries. For some time now I have been training them to make their own the anxieties and lives of our missionary colleagues. We exchange frequent letters as communities that listen to and love each other. And my people are now familiar with the usages and customs of the peoples out there, and they with ours. I cannot tell you, Your Eminence, what great blessings we have received, as we share the sufferings of those communities, which though poor are rich and though in need of everything so joyfully receive and live out the gospel message!"

"But no one save you, Lord, can know the generosity of those who with tears sow your word of truth in distant lands. And you alone can reward these dear missionaries of yours, who have given or are giving everything: time, energies, life itself—you alone can reward them with the joy of having given this Church of yours a more flourishing future." Every vocation is a life spent, body and soul, in a cause: the cause of Christ, who does not follow set times in bestowing the gift of faith. Totally dedicated missionaries are the Church's great treasure. Their witness should be held in special honor and should serve as a point of reference (but one that is really taken seriously) by all the various and extremely valuable kinds of volunteers who help keep alive the exchanges between the new churches and the churches with ancient traditions behind them.

One example of such exchanges is the African missions of our diocese in Zambia and Cameroon. These missions are not so much a source of pride or a proof of the lively missionary spirit of our diocese, as they are an experience that can enrich our Milanese community if the latter is prepared to allow itself to be educated through a lively pastoral exchange. Also, our Diocesan Missionary Center deserves special thanks and encouragement. Its widespread work in the parishes is extremely important.

In Dialogue with the Indifferent and the Distant

I often have a strange experience: when I am far from home, I feel a nostalgia for it and seem able to think more clearly about local problems, whereas when I am at home I feel almost smothered. This is explained by our close attachment to our daily duties, as well as by our anxious desire not to be crushed by the monotony of the ordinary but to broaden our horizons and our own souls.

The horizons of the universal Church, and the creative Spirit of God: these are what give dimension and inspiration to every parochial community. The churches in the missions can help us discover a new pastoral style for use here at home, a style based on the generosity of God and on his fatherhood that knows no boundaries. Boundaries exist in fact and can be too constraining, especially today when what is enclosed is a little flock, more of whom are outside than inside. Moreover, those far off are now close to home, and the house is not always a heart that beats like the heart of Christ.

A young priest was unburdening his heart: "Missionaries go over there to evangelize and, admittedly, experience many difficulties and make many sacrifices. But do they not find there, at least in various populations, a soil to work that is rich in values and filled with great expectations? What about us here? We are afraid of losing possessions that are now depleted, and in the process we lose what would be a real gain: the trust and credibility that would be ours if we were more concerned to enter into dialogue with all, whether near or far from us in the faith." [Typically,] these indifferent or distant folk are no longer thought important by us because we think them confused with their mishmash of rites and magical practices, occasional exercises of faith and hybrid forms of secularism.

Perhaps we ought to conduct fewer surveys and sociological analyses and try instead a more honest examination of conscience as disciples of Christ and Christian communities. "You, O Christ, have already said everything we need, but your every word strikes fear into us!" Fear then begets rigidity, inflexibility, and reliance on set ways. We close ranks to defend ourselves. Fear of making mistakes becomes the psychosis of those who are mistaken. And what does Christ say to me here?: "Every soul cost me my blood, and it takes so little to alienate and lose one and thus to discredit the Church and my redemption." Prudence and love are needed, courage and love, expectation and love, respect and love. "Who knows the secrets of the human heart if not you, O God? And why are we so harsh and condemnatory, while you are so good and forgiving?"

"But I make every effort to understand and keep close to those who have little to do with the Church!" said my colleague, who looked at me as though pleading with me: "What more ought I have done?" Beloved, I do not have the words with which to tell you how deeply it matters to me that ours should be a missionary community, open to dialogue and respectful of all, especially those who for countless different reasons have trouble keeping pace with a more authentic faith. What more can be done? If you have the love of Christ within you, you will find opportunities for approaching the indifferent and the distant. Isn't love creative by its very nature? Pray and reflect. Reread what I have written elsewhere, especially in the letter *In principio la Parola* (In the Beginning the Word).

Here I would like to say only one thing to you or, better, repeat it until you are sick of it: You must allow the most varied needs to touch you and stimulate your faith; if you do, you will find the right way of approaching, listening to, and entering into dialogue with all. Being able to listen is the first step to dialogue. The other must then listen, and then I must listen again, until a mutual respect and sincere friendship has been established. The Lord will see to the rest.

"How we hurry about, Lord! But doesn't education mean loving patience? Isn't that how you love me, O Christ?"

Despite continual complaints we priests have not yet realized how unaffected the ordinary people are by our sermons and by the official documents of the Church. Yet they live honorable and sacrificial lives and feel the need of a simple word, of friendly relations, of a priest who knows how to listen. We should either deal with these Christians in this manner and try to keep a continual dialogue going with them, or we should retire to private life! Yes, we must keep dialogue going. We must never quench even the weakest spark of light. And dialogue, remember, does not mean only telling the other, after listening to him or her: "You're right! Continue as you are!" An evangelizing dialogue means saying to the other: "You may have countless reasons for dissenting from the Church in many matters. I am here to listen to you. But I am also here to tell you that Christ loves you and is waiting for you. He understands you and he waits for you. He knows your heart and he does not coerce you at all. He does not want you to belong to him if you have to be forced. And if you persist in your present ways, at least do not close the doors and windows of your heart to the voice of God!"

Only have patience, a great deal of patience, the patience of God, and you will see that sooner or later people will again believe in the gospel and give credence to the Church. Our task meanwhile is really to live according to the word of God and to trust in the integrity of so many people who are indeed confused about the faith for numerous reasons unknown to us. It can be easy and even a duty to judge facts, but consciences are in God's hands. And while the law of God judges the actions and behavior of each individual, it never loses its pedagogical function of leading wrongdoers to repentance. We can never forget that law always has a corrective purpose: it educates people to a better life, to conversion, to salvation. This is true also of the law of the Church. "How many people, Lord, have become indifferent or alienated due to a law gone dead in their hearts? And you, Father, did you not anxiously await the return of the prodigal son?" Why then should we close the door in so many situations and leave souls in agony to die without hope?

Finally, an invitation to you, the believing, living community: do not think only of yourselves, your community obligations, your growth and maturity amid brothers and sisters who share the same beliefs and the same ideals. Open yourself to all. Get involved in the various areas of social life in your surroundings. Widen the range of your concerns to include all the needs of the local community. Organize affairs at which those representing the various political or social or cultural trends can meet as human beings and citizens. Keep alive a calm dialogue with all the forces at work in the region. This will not be easy. Any dialogue requires patience, sincerity, and honesty of intentions; the ability to meet without demanding pride of place for ourselves, our ideas, our religious or political creed. Anything in common can be a starting point. It is important to try.

The Voiceless

There are missions in distant lands and there is a mission here at home that must deal with those who are distant as far as the practice of religion is concerned. There is another reality besides the one familiar to us: that of those who are distant because they are marginalized, those therefore who live at the edge of our human and Christian attention or sensitivity. More than a few simple thoughts are needed in order to speak properly of this whole sphere, which today seems to be spreading and marked by growing loneliness and massiveness. Our diocese certainly cannot be considered seriously unaffected from this scene, given its broad presence and noteworthy commitment. In addition, did we not also hold a great diocesan conference on caring service in November, 1986, at the end of the pastoral program which I outlined in the letter *Farsi prossimo* ("Becoming a Neighbor")?

Linking this "becoming a neighbor" with the missionary dimension of the Church and of each local community, I would like to say how very important it is not to forget the perspective opened up for us in the well-known parable of the Good Samaritan. "And who is my neighbor?" a doctor of the law asks Jesus. The teacher answers like a real teacher, by telling an upsetting story. He seems to be answering the question that has been asked, but in reality he is provoking the Jewish theologian by forcing him to focus his attention not so much on "Who is my neighbor?" as on the way in which the Samaritan "became a neighbor." "Which of these three, do you think, was a neighbor to the man who fell into the hands of the robbers?" The theologian asnwered, "The one who showed him mercy." And Jesus said to him, "Go and do likewise" (Luke 10:36-37).

"Which of these three?"—that is Christ's question, and the answer is already given in the action of the Samaritan, who sees, stops, gives first aid, looks for help, and concerns himself beyond the minimum required. There is always something *more* for those who love and who feel the urgency of Christ's love. Every pastoral program should allow the Spirit to breathe as and where it wills, in every circumstance; it should leave freedom for some undefined "more" in every need that arises. "If you, Lord, are the Unpredictable One, why should we try to restrain you?"

"I am certainly shaken, and my soul is saddened, at the frightening sight of burning problems and human tragedies that truly wring the heart!" I saw that this colleague was bitter at not being close to so many unfortunates of our day. "Your Eminence," he continued, "in my little area there are no real tragedies, or they are so exceptional that it is really difficult not to be aware of them and to do something if needed. But how can I myself become a neighbor? Should I perhaps be afflicted because I am in a sense fortunate? Should I leave there and go elsewhere?" The problem, as I have already written, is not so much to do, at whatever cost, something that will make me feel like "a neighbor," or to try to solve all by myself the whole range of marginalizations—physical and psychic handicaps, drug addiction, AIDS, immigration of other races, and so on— that are causing increasing alarm in some circles of our diocese. These are big problems that call for special attention, specific kinds of intervention, and programs of highly specialized assistance, above and beyond noteworthy but sporadic kinds of caring activity. Besides, there is no lack of many individual crises, and here each of us is directly challenged.

Now, dear colleague, I want to tell you something important: The entire diocese and the universal Church, each in its near or distant reality, should be present in the heart of each believer and each Christian community, be this large or small. Each should also make their own the really large problems. The efforts to solve these problems should be supported by all, no matter whether or not they affect us directly. Tomorrow it may be you who is called to deal with such a situation, at the center of the storm or in hot spots further afield, and you may wish you could accuse of absenteeism those who, like you today, are content to remain quietly in their own little corner.

There are situations that call for common Christian attention in the form of awareness and of moral and economic support; these are to be given in a great spirit of faith that makes us look upon one another as brothers and sisters, all members of a single community, be we as large as the diocese or even as universal as the Church. "Every person has a task, Lord. The important thing is not simply to exist here or there, with this or that problem. The important thing is to feel ourselves united in your name, with hearts open as yours was on the cross."

Finally, dear colleague, I want to emphasize one further point. In your present circumstances, however limited, you must have a great missionary outlook, even as you deal with problems thought to be of little moment. You say you do not have the time and energy to think of those with greater problems than yours and to involve your community in them. You cannot commit yourself any further to the task of vitalizing your deanery? But there is no question of doing something, unless the opportunity or some great occasion arises. The real issue is one of life-style. You must think of yourself as a missionary in every aspect of your life: preaching, hearing confessions, administering the sacraments, approaching people, holding dialogue with all. "My God, how many hidden handicaps there are! How are we to discover them and give help and support?" The need is not for great deeds but for little daily gestures of attention, for that great spirit of faith and love that inspires our entire priestly existence and forms the Christian community to be missionary, here, everywhere, and always. "Which of these three?" It was not the priest or the Levite, but a Samaritan!

Il Segno 12 (December 1990)

Chapter 12

Before rewriting the fifth section of "Departure for Emmaus," I would like to tell of an experience I had at the Cathedral during the last Missionary Vigil on October 20, 1990. During the celebration I found the heart of today's missionary problem becoming clearer to me.

Why Go to the Missions?

Those gathered were talking about the Third World, its needs, the injustices of the West, international debt, the exploitation of raw materials by Europe, and so on. I was listening carefully and asking myself: Are these really the reasons why people leave for the missions? If these were the only reasons, our men and women missionaries would be going as teachers or social workers. And what has all this to do with the crucifix that will shortly be given to each? When there is question of development and environment, those directly challenged are not priests or missionaries but all of the laity, all persons of good will, especially all the volunteers of whatever faith. These are great communal responsibilities that weigh on the entire human race and that spur individuals to help one another. Knowledge of Jesus and the cross leads us to see in our suffering brother or sister the face of Jesus, and it spurs us on to "become neighbors." But is this really enough to express the deeper reasons for the departure of these missionary men and women to whom the crucifix will shortly be given? A more specific motive is needed for going to the missions, and it has to do not only with problems of health, environment, justice, development, or the economy, but with the ignorance of Jesus Christ under which many suffer, and with the determination that the God of whom these missionaries are enamored may be known! It is this love of God that makes people missionaries! It is the joy which the priceless pearl gives them that makes them want others to know it. It is the joy of the gospel that drives them to the missions. It is their wonder at the good news they have received that makes them spontaneously speak of it to others.

When we seem to have found an effective medicine for our bodies, a means of fighting some widespread disease, we do not hesitate to talk about it enthusiastically to others as soon as an occasion offers. In like manner, the missionary impulse springs from the joy of having found a treasure and the desire of sharing it with those whom we wish well. An intense love of the Lord and a desire that he be known opens us also to a spacious and astonishing vision of human dignity, so that we want everyone else to make the same discovery. The words of John Paul II in his first encyclical, *Redemptor hominis*, are relevant here:

> In reality, the name for that deep amazement at man's worth and dignity is the Gospel, that is to say: the Good News. It is also called Christianity. This amazement determines the Church's mission in the world and, perhaps even more so, *in the modern world*. This amazement, which is also a conviction and a certitude—at its deepest root it is the certainty of faith, but in a hidden and mysterious way it vivifies every aspect of authentic humanism—is closely connected with Christ. . . . Unceasingly contemplating the whole of Christ's mystery, the Church knows with all the certainty of faith that the Redemption that took place through the cross has definitively restored his dignity to man and given back meaning to his life in the world, a meaning that was lost to a considerable extent because of sin. And for that reason, the Redemption was accomplished in the paschal mystery, leading through the cross and death to resurrection.

The Church's fundamental function in every age and particularly in ours is to direct man's gaze, to point the awareness and experience of the whole of humanity toward the mystery of God, to help all men to be familiar with the profundity of the Redemption taking place in Christ Jesus (no. 10).

In this passage we see restored the balance of values and motives that impel men and women, today as yesterday and always, to go as missionaries both among distant peoples and among our own.

Let Us Speak of the Word

I was making preparations for a retreat I was to conduct. The theme was one proposed by many persons and, in addition, urgently required by the pastoral needs of the diocese. My concern was to focus on some basic truths, dwell at length on these, and get them across in a more incisive way. At this time I was also feeling the same difficulties as so many of my colleagues. How was I to make the message of Christ more alive? How was I to convey this message to the real world in which those who would be listening to me were living? I was distracted by the thought of the countless aversions people have to listening and the question of why speech has become anonymous, has lost its effectiveness, its almost magical power to capture attention. I recalled a question or challenge someone had posed to me: "The Church has always had two very effective ways of operating: the word of God and charity to the needy. Will the Church of today be able to use them with equal power and conviction?" We know the great challenges that Christian charity continually faces at the present time. But we are also aware of the difficulties, which in a way are today much more serious, that the proclamation of God's word must overcome. For this reason there flashed through my mind an idea for the retreat: the theme would address the proclamation of the word. This is a matter of very great importance, given the fact that the word of God precedes mission. "Lord, your word is a word that liberates. How can we keep it hushed up?"

"How are we to announce this word to the people of today, who seem anything but well disposed to receive it?" The elderly priest who put this question to me was not at all resigned to remaining silent, but he did show that he felt the full weight of the hostility with which he met, sometimes even among his own practicing faithful: "Just think, Your Eminence. There was a time when the people stayed even for hours listening to our sermons! But today? Go a minute overtime, and someone flies off the handle! Then, too, who does any good reading nowadays? There are indeed religious books, and some of them are even too beautiful: books that capture the eye but not always the heart." This outburst reminded me of many truths, but of one in particular. People today no longer have time to listen or to read, but only to look. Is there an unconscious rejection at work here, a hostility stemming from the excessive wear and tear caused by empty and inconclusive words? A felt need of self-defense? Life is so stressful that people do not even want to think, and as a result the mind instinctively refuses to enter into itself. What with empty words and anxieties that wear it down, the soul amuses itself with diversions. "Lord, how are we to give them a taste for your mystery of grace?"

"And do you realize, Your Eminence, that today it is difficult for us to listen even to one another? To grasp one another's meaning? Even though we use the same words and the same tongue? Even brothers and sisters in the faith? I feel bitter when, after a sermon delivered with great warmth, I hear some fellow tell me: 'I was really pleased by what you said there, especially . . .,' and I have to look at him while feeling tempted to clear up his misunderstanding: 'But, my dear man, I did not say that at all!'" "Hostility, indifference, painful misunderstandings: what else is there, O Christ, to seal off your word?"

My dear brother evangelizer, the word of God has always found obstacles in its way. Is not the path of freedom always a costly one? And the wound that bleeds the most is the failure to be accepted or understood. Is it not madness to reject light or freedom? And yet we live in a world in which madness is at home, if it be true that people prefer darkness to the light and instead of being free prefer to keep their hearts and minds pinned down by trifles. We should not be surprised. Truth has always had a hard time gaining acceptance, precisely because truth sets free. And Freedom wants freedom. It is respectful, therefore, and knows how to wait. On the other hand, the evil one is not helped if human beings use their minds and discover him who is eternal.

It is certainly frightening—how very much so!—that a blessed child of God should not know where truth is and where error is, and should venture with closed eyes on the downward slope of the most deceptive relativism. It is frightening because the stakes here are the person's life, his or her eternal destiny, the destiny of all humankind. "My God, the good of human beings is here and they reject it; the darkness approaches, and they run to meet it! But your word does not give up; it is a seed that dies, dies so many times, but in order to bear fruit in even the hardest soil."

There I was, caught up in these distractions, at a time when I had to draft some thoughts for the retreat. One thought still kept me far from my task, or, rather, was an indispensable preamble to the task: "Does not proclaiming your message, O God, mean first of all contemplating it?" Here precisely is the secret of the effectiveness of our preaching and of all catechesis. It is not a mere human message that we speak: it is the truth of Christ, the supreme message, the mystery of life. First of all, therefore, we must take possession of it, we must love it with our whole soul. We must feel it throb within us, with all its challenges and all its urging, and then communicate it with faith and deepest love.

Our people take notice when we speak from the heart, that is, when the message quivers with life within us, laying hold first of our heart and our mind and then our speech. "And you, incarnate Word, are here, as always, ready to meet us and inviting us to the great dialogue."

What of Catechesis?

How are we to preach this word to the people of today? The question keeps recurring like a refrain every time the question of catechesis comes up. I feel like answering: "Take the gospel and meditate at length on those wonderful pages that tell of Jesus' meetings with individuals of his time." These scenes are like marvelous paintings: the more we look at them, the more we admire them without ever wearying. There is always something new to be discovered; no stroke is merely decorative; everything is more eloquent than any word could be. "But does not your word, O Lord, contain and express more than human art can?"

These passages of the gospel are more than wonderful paintings to be hung on the walls of the house. They are encounters with Christ that still come to life again and again. In them the magnificent pedagogy of the divine Teacher is at work.

Christ is our model, our ideal, pedagogical ideal that has no match. It is for us to compare ourselves with him if we want to understand something of our humaness and how we can come to grips with the human person in its deepest desire for the infinite. Dear evangelizer, are you likewise finding it difficult to approach the people of our day, to talk seriously with them about God and freedom, and to preach and catechize? Try taking a passage of the gospel—Jesus' meeting with Zacchaeus, or the Samaritan woman, or so many others—and you will make important discoveries. Above all, you will discover, on one side, a certain heartfelt interior uneasiness, a deep thirst, a desire for something beyond the realities of the moment. On the other side, in Christ, you will be struck by the expectation that turns into a presence, a closeness, sometimes a challenge, and, then, a disconcerting answer. "I seek you, Lord, and you always let yourself be found. You seek me, everywhere, and incite me to seek you."

It is always Christ who causes me to desire him, he who waits for the moment when my yearning for the infinite, my desires for peace, my painful doubts and challenging questions, cross paths with his waiting self and his saving word.

"Not even obstinate silences or stubborn rejections are enough to discourage you, O Christ!" You will go on to observe that, meeting after meeting, Christ never repeats himself. There is always something new in his look, in his conversation, in the way he incites to dialogue. But, then, is love not unpredictable, extraordinary, out of the common, creative, personal? This is why I urge you to linger over each page of the gospel, for you will find there all the answers to your problems, in all possible situations.

Il Segno 1 (January 1991)

Chapter 13

As I make the rounds of the parishes I often hear a good many whys: Why are we seeing an ever increasing confusion of ideas? Why can we not manage to grasp what real freedom is? Why has the idea become widespread among many Christians, to the point of becoming almost a slogan, that in the final analysis we can just live and let live and that it does not matter much whether or not so many people are on wrong paths, provided it is their own decision? "Why all this, Lord? What do you, with your idea of freedom, think of it all? Where is your word?"

I frequently sense a fear in the minds of good people, that all reference to the word of God has been lost. People's thinking is governed by the latest trend. Everything is good provided it does not attack one's own right to privacy. If so many people still allow God to enter their lives, they do it with a vague sentimentality that permits them, as need arises, to justify every weakness and distortion of conscience.

Let Us Return to the Word

"Well, then," I answer, "if this is indeed the reality of the moment, let us return with greater faith to the word of God and proclaim it once more in all its freshness and power!" "The thicker the fog, Lord, the greater need we have of your light."

Among the various forms of the ministry of the word, there is one which has the specific purpose of enlightening the minds of believers so that they may have a more mature understanding of the demands of their faith: this form is catechesis. As the Italian Episcopal Conference says in its document "The Renewal of Catechesis," "The Church develops the basic proclamation of God's word by means of catechesis; it seeks thereby to direct human beings on their journey to faith, from the conferral or rediscovery of baptism to the fullness of Christian life." The work of catechesis must be done all the more fervently the more society is fragmented, lacking in spiritual motivation, living at an unchanged plateau, prisoner of a false idea of freedom and pluralism, haunted by fears, and jealously attached to its little world of things enjoyed and to be enjoyed.

This work is needed precisely because at times we seem to be crying out, like John the Baptist, in a desolate wilderness. "The voice of one crying out in the wilderness: 'Prepare the way of the Lord'" (Matt 3:3). "But, Savior, haven't you already come? Have you not already met each of us?" Let us not weary of crying out to all that Christ, indeed, has already come and is waiting for us to receive him. He has come and he is coming. And see, these modern men and women are still people who have their hopes and want to see the Savior who is coming and who is passing by. Even if the expectation now seems to be declining and people do not seem to raise their eyes beyond earthly desires, there is all the greater need of a voice that cries out: "All flesh shall see the salvation of God!" (Luke 3:6).

But How Are We to Do This?

I often hear the objection: "How are we going to catechize all these confused people? Very few come to our parish meetings, and always the same few. And they are more than mature. There is no time for catechizing during Sunday Masses; it's already more than we can expect if we put in a good word concerning the gospel and get people to listen. And in the afternoons what is left of the famous Sunday schools that educated entire generations of the faithful? Yes, there are times when there is a good turnout—for example, of the parents of children preparing for first communion or confirmation. Yet it is precisely here that the whole situation becomes clear: you need only say a few words to realize how little sense of Christian responsibility today's parents have and how they judge faith and Church from the usual viewpoint of laicist prejudices. Your Eminence, it's fine to say that we must also listen to the needs of the people. But would it not be more expedient in this day and age to make these wretched Christians realize that they must listen first and foremost to the word of God?"

This is indeed the priority of all priorities. We must educate people to listen to the word. It is the word that educates, and the word that judges and frees. We do not have to invent it. We must take this word and introduce it into the minds and hearts of the people and of each individual in all his or her historical reality. Let us invent new forms, provided the message always conveys the word of God, the entire word of truth, namely, that God really wills my good and offers me the fullest salvation. All things can be of service, even the most unexpected occasions, for announcing this extraordinary message to all. Every occasion demands attention and respect, all the more so when the word is being spoken to hearts that are uncertain or indifferent or not very well disposed. Let us also reevaluate our many now-and-then meetings on special occasions (funerals, marriages, baptisms, and so on) and try to devise the best conditions for catechizing these "momentary" Christians. "Here, again, it is you, O Christ, who teach everyone a truly missionary style. Your gospel is rich in these occasional meetings that leave an indelible mark."

Everything can be of service in catechizing. But let us not be satisfied with a minimum, while at the same time not allowing ourselves to be fooled by quantity. The missionary style aims at quality above all. Let us see to it that every contact and even the simple giving of religious information conveys a view of the Church as open to today's world, in the most authentic gospel spirit, and a view of the diocese or parish that enables people to glimpse the heart of the Father who loves all and is searching out all. "The real face of the Church is your face, O Christ; it is a mystery of grace that requires the greatest attention and respect."

But let us not neglect a more systematic, ordinary catechesis. Let us go back to the catechetical school in a serious and organized way. "Lord, give us your word so that we may have a new awareness of the mystery of grace. Help us to be listeners, like Mary of Bethany." It is necessary, therefore, once again to tackle the problem of catechesis in the parish with courage and great prophetic insight; of a catechesis that will enable the community truly to walk in the light of the gospel. We must find utterly new ways of bathing the present apathy in the light of Christ, of helping Christians discover the real saving mystery, of enabling the communities to experience the joy of proclaiming the freedom of Christ to today's world. "Lord, why do these young people and adults flee your light? How do they manage to endure the mist in their hearts?"

We can stay debating the matter for hours on end, for whole days, months, and years, and the reasons given for the crisis in catechesis will always leave us dissatisfied, unless we decide once and for all to put more faith in the word that saves. This is the starting point for a more incisive and persuasive reevangelization. If the word of God is no longer heard, why put all the blame on present-day society? Is it really the fault of young people and adults that catechesis is no longer a part of their Christian practice? "What of us, your disciples, Lord? What place do we give to your word?"

Let us try to ask ourselves sincerely: Do these young people and these adults really reject the word of God, or are they simply no longer drawn by our tired, muddled, cold, and lifeless catechesis? I am more than convinced that the people of our day in particular have a thirst for God, for the infinite, for a hope that does not fade at the first death of desires or troubles. When did these living beings ever not desire a deeper good beyond purely earthly joys? As for the anxiety people experience today, their great restlessness, the discontents of society, and the various kinds of violence, are these not rebellions against the only too evident limitations of the human? If the people of today are indeed uncertain and full of longing, if they are made up of mire mingled with trembling spirit, why do we leave them with the thirst that burns in their hearts? "But there is only one word that quenches the soul's thirst and its burning desires for the infinite. And why do we, O Christ, repeat this word of yours without any interior conviction?"

Catechizing Children

We take it to be mistaken when people accuse our religion of being "stuff good only for children"; on the other hand, if we look about, we see ourselves surrounded by a great many children. If these children come to us, is it not because they at least feel the attraction exerted by a message of hope and life? But at the same time the question arises: Have not a good many of them been brought for catechism in order that they may be able to receive the sacraments of Christian initiation, rites which the parents still value because of strong traditional custom? What matters more to the parents of these children: that their children be instructed in the faith, or that they have an opportunity for a beautiful ritual celebration? "But, Lord, what meaning does the sacrament have apart from your word of life?"

Sometimes I have the impression that even some of these little ones are already indifferent and distant because their parent's faith is so minimal. If the children lack the support of a truly Christian family, what is the point of evangelizing them? Is there not a danger that they will approach the catechism confused, indifferent, and at best seeking some points of information? This is not an inviting picture. But if this is at least one face of reality, what are we to do to change it?

It is important to look at the situation as it really is and to try something new in methods and forms by establishing family groups and by developing more mature catechists. Rather than create an elite that will enable us to enjoy a more consoling faith, we must try to form missionary communities for various levels of action: from the catechesis of little children to catechesis for young people and adults. "We are always engaged in mission, Lord, especially where the soil has become hard and resistant to the seed of your word." If the soil is stubborn, we must give it more attention and plow it more lovingly. It needs sun, rain, and a great deal of care. In our catechesis we must focus on the substance of the gospel and make this as clear as possible. But very gradually, with patience and understanding.

When we catechize these little ones, let us not forget those farther off, I mean their parents. It is here that the missionary spirit urges us into calm dialogue. This may even be the first, and at times the only, chance to approach them. A community grows if it has the unwearying patience for a creative reevangelization that is strongly inspired by faith in the power of the saving word. "Where are we to start?" someone may ask. I would give a summary answer that has already been given in the Italian Episcopal Conference's basic document on the fundamentals of catechesis in Italy. The question is not so much one of *catechisms* as it is one of *catechesis* and, even more, one of Christian communities that listen to the word of God and put it into practice in an evangelical, that is, missionary spirit. If at least the more committed people in a parish felt the need of a lively, weekly catechesis, would we not already have missionaries ready to inspire the growth of the community, from the youngest to the oldest?

Il Segno 2 (February 1991)

Chapter 14

These articles in *Il Segno* follow the structure of "Departure from Emmaus," but they also seek to record impressions and events having to do with the theme of "mission" and "missionary" at the present time. I wish therefore to begin this installment with some first thoughts on the new "missionary" encyclical of John Paul II: *Redemptoris Missio* ("Mission of the Redeemer"). The encyclical is dated December 7, 1990, the twenty-fifth anniversary of the conciliar Decree *Ad gentes* on the Church's missionary activity, and was published in January, 1991.

An Authoritative Reminder

The subtitle of the papal encyclical makes clear its purpose: "On the Permanent Validity of the Church's Missionary Mandate." The words presuppose that our times have seen the emergence of doubts or difficulties regarding the missionary mandate that has driven the Church's history since the beginning and in particular has fostered a major effort of missionary activity in Africa and Asia during the last century and a half.

The encyclical acknowledges that "today we face a religious situation which is extremely varied and changing. People are on the move; social and religious realities which were once clear and well-defined are today increasingly complex" (no. 32). This has led to new ways of looking at things and also to questions about the "missions." The Pope notes that there is, for example, "a certain hesitation to use the term 'missions' and 'missionaries,' which are considered obsolete and as having negative historical connotations. People prefer to use instead the noun 'mission' in the singular and the adjective 'missionary' to describe all the Church's activities. This uneasiness," he goes on to say, "denotes a real change, one which has certain positive aspects. The so-called return or 'repatriation' of the missions into the Church's mission, the insertion of missiology into ecclesiology and the integration of both areas into the Trinitarian plan of salvation have given a fresh impetus to missionary activity itself, which is not considered a marginal task for the Church but is situated at the center of her life as a fundamental commitment to the whole people of God" (no. 32).

But, while acknowledging this praiseworthy development, the Pope forcefully asserts that this does "not preclude the existence of a specific mission *ad gentes*" and "not only does not exclude, but actually requires that there be persons who have a specific vocation to be 'lifelong missionaries *ad gentes*" (ibid.).

The fundamental theme of the encyclical is therefore the mission to those who have never heard the gospel proclaimed, and today these are still the vast majority of the human race.

But the Pope also takes into account the case of "missionary work" at home, the kind of mission with which I am more specifically concerned in this rewriting of "Departure from Emmaus." In general, the principles which the Pope sets down for the missionary work of the Church apply also to our diocesan situation. I want to call particular attention to some points.

First of all, let me consider a basic principle. To the question, Why mission? the Pope replies: "Mission is an issue of faith, an accurate indicator of our faith in Christ and His love for us" (no. 11). Here we have the heart of the matter and the reason why, immediately following on a year dedicated to "The Eucharist as Center of the Community" (1983, the year of the Eucharistic Congress), I proclaimed a year dedicated to "mission" (1983–84, the year of "Departure from Emmaus"). I wrote at the time: "We need to discover the missionary outcome of the path of contemplation, listening, and Eucharist which we have thus far been travelling" (that is, during the years 1980–83, when I wrote in succession the letters entitled *La dimensione contemplativa della vita [The Contemplative Dimension of Life], In principio la Parola [In the Beginning the Word]*, and *Attirerò tutti a me [I Will Draw All to Myself]*). The missionary thrust was inherent in all of these and found expression in the title given to the Eucharistic Congress: "L'Eucaristia al centro della communità e della sua missione" ("The Eucharist, Center of the Community and Its Mission"). I remember having insisted on this title at the meeting of the Italian Episcopal Conference, in preference to other impressive titles that had been suggested, such as "Jesus is Lord" or "Eucharist and Community." In my view, the title ought to contain a practical program for the life of Christian communities in the 1980s, and the idea of mission could not be absent from such a title. Now, at the beginning of the 1990s, the Pope has confirmed my approach.

Another passage of the new papal encyclical that is very relevant to us addresses the various conceptions of the relation between the kingdom, on the one hand, and Christ and the Church, on the other. The Pope censures a reductive view of the kingdom which he calls "anthropocentric": "In this view, the kingdom tends to become something completely human and secularized; what counts are programs and struggles for a liberation which is socioeconomic, political, and even cultural, but within a horizon that is closed to the transcendent" (no. 17).

But even some "kingdom-centered" views do not avoid ambiguity. These are attractive because they rightly stress "the image of a Church which is not concerned about herself, but which is totally concerned with bearing witness to and serving the kingdom. It is a 'Church for others' just as Christ is the 'man for others'" (ibid.). The negative side of this view emerges when its proponents think they can do without Christ, the excuse being that "Christ cannot be understood by those who lack Christian faith, whereas different peoples, cultures, and religions are capable of finding common ground in the one divine reality, by whatever name it is called" (ibid.).

The result is a vague "theocentrism" that plays down the mystery of Christ; it likes to talk about "creation" but is silent about the mystery of redemption, and it undervalues the Church (ibid.). In contrast, the Pope asserts that the kingdom of God as known to us from revelation "cannot be detached either from Christ or from the Church" (no. 18).

The Areas of Mission

I want to call attention, in addition, to some passages of the encyclical that describe the scope or sphere of mission and include those which are closer to home for us. The encyclical distinguishes three situations. First of all, there is the area in which missionary activity in the most proper sense is carried on, namely, among those groups of human beings who do not yet know Christ and his gospel. Second, there are the solidly established and fervent Christian communities that bear witness to the gospel in their surroundings and have a commitment to the universal mission. In these communities the Church carries on its activity and pastoral care. Third, the Pope mentions an intermediate situation, to be found particularly in countries which have long been Christian but in which whole groups of the baptized have lost a living sense of faith. What is needed in these cases is a "new evangelization" or a "reevangelization."

We recognize this third situation as our own. That is why I have strongly insisted, on other occasions, that our situation cannot be described simply as that of a secularized world. Different ways of life coexist among us; for some the faith is still sincerely lived, for others it is practically absent. This makes our situation a special one and different from that of fifty or a hundred years ago when those engaged in pastoral care could assume at least an apparent unanimity in faith. Our situation is not one in which we start from zero, as in a first evangelization, nor one in which we need only cultivate and promote what is already there, as used to be the case in "Christendom." The thing that makes our activity as a Church especially difficult here (and makes it, in some respects, more complicated than in the mission *ad gentes*) is that we must move back and forth between pastoral efforts in regard to those "near" to us and attention and commitment to those who are "distant." This is both our trial and our joy, the constantly resurfacing problem of our existence as Church in Europe at the end of the second millennium.

While the Pope is concerned in his encyclical more particularly with the first of three above-named situations, he too calls attention to the fact that "the boundaries between pastoral care of the faithful, new evangelization, and specific missionary activity are not clearly definable, and it is unthinkable to create barriers between them or to put them into watertight compartments" (no. 34). The same point is made in those passages in which the Pope goes on to define more closely the various parameters of the mission *ad gentes*. He mentions not only territorial limits, that is, territories in which Christ has not yet been sufficiently proclaimed, but also "new worlds and new social phenomena" and "cultural sectors: the modern equivalents of the Areopagus." Just as in Athens St. Paul went to the Areopagus, which was the cultural center of the day, so today the gospel must be proclaimed in the places where culture is being shaped and transmitted (see no. 37).

The Pope refers in particular to the world of communications, "which is unifying humanity and turning it into what is known as a 'global village'" (ibid.). We may therefore claim that the Pope has confirmed our choice when we dedicated the two-year period 1989–1991 to "communication," a period for making explicit the focus on mission set forth in "Departure from Emmaus." The Pope reminds us that it is not enough to use one or another of the communications media to spread the Christian message; "it is also necessary to integrate that message into the 'new culture' created by modern communications. This is a complex issue, since the 'new culture' originates not just from whatever context is eventually expressed, but from the very fact that there exist new ways of communicating, with new languages, new techniques and a new psychology" (ibid.). It is precisely this theme that we are trying to deal with in the diocese, both this year with *Effatà* ("Be Opened!") and next year with an application of *Effatà* to the worlds of mass communication.

The Pope reminds us that the "Areopagus" is present in many places throughout the modern world, toward which the missionary activity of the Church must likewise be directed; for example, "commitment to peace, development and the liberation of peoples; the rights of individuals and peoples, especially those of minorities; the advancement of women and children; safeguarding the created world" (no. 37). The dramatic events that took place in the Persian Gulf area remind us of the degree to which the service of peace and justice is part of our mandate and what destruction of the good things of creation follows upon violations of peace and right.

I have spent more time than I anticipated in recalling some points of the encyclical; I have done so because I think they are very relevant to the subject of these articles. Each of you will be able to read *Redemptoris Missio* for yourselves and meditate on it. By way of conclusion to this article, I shall simply recall a few ideas from "Departure from Emmaus" on the catechist as witness to the faith. This is one way of living the missionary calling of our Church.

The Catechist as Witness

I sometimes hear the question, What can we do to gain a better hearing? Should we too perhaps organize more meetings of an athletic or cultural kind? Indeed, everything good can be an occasion of grace, and nothing should be neglected that enables us to put in a good word. The word of God, however, has a style of its own: unmatched, original, unique. This word requires prayer, interior silence, profound attention. Christ himself made use of every occasion to meet people, but the meeting turned into a dialogue of hearts, richly human, decisive, leading to action. The action was sometimes acceptance and sometimes rejection, but it was always decisive.

"Christ, you spoke to the soul and involved the whole of the person's humanity." There are countless occasions for us to create or take advantage of in a community that is passive or practices but little. But we must not be content with merely occasional meetings, no matter how numerous. We must move on from there to build and foster convictions. "Your message, Lord, demands this. It is a message aimed at freedom and the journey of freedom." A present-day community that finds it hard to keep pace with a faith lived to the full needs various kinds of attention. All do not march to the same drum. Nonetheless, it is a mistake and countereducational to hinder the pace of all because of the hesitancy of some. Admittedly, we must not run for the sake of running, but we must indeed walk on, looking ahead and aiming at improvement. Indeed, we look back at those who lag, but only to help them, or even to prick them and thus stimulate them to do more.

At this point I can hear someone saying, "But people come only to amuse themselves, and as soon as we propose something that means greater commitment, they have all sorts of excuses and absent themselves. What a wearying task it is at times to get even our most practicing Christians into a discussion: they don't want to know about the catechism or anything else, and to make them come you've got to grab them by the neck!" My dear challenger, the situation is certainly not a rosy one for any of us, and the complaints that come in from the various parts of the diocese serve to prove the seriousness of the phenomenon.

Let us try to think things out a bit. What do we really ask of the believing laity who surround us? What value do we set on them? Are we satisfied with a collaboration of service alone, because in the final analysis we're comfortable with that? Do we educate them to an ever greater discovery of the gift of faith in all its missionary richness? Every community has great energies latent in it; we must assess them as quickly as possible.

"Lord, grant these believers of ours more confidence in themselves and in the mystery in which they believe. And grant us, O Christ, more confidence in them and in their great capacities."

And you, dear brother or sister in the faith, do not look at me as though you were asking incredulously, What good can we laity do for this kingdom of God? Today it is the Church itself that calls you to a highly responsible, not to say necessary task. It is true, we are in a difficult situation. But the Church needs you because you, the layperson, are important. Your mission in the Church is an important one. Do not continue judging the past, or even the present that is still closed off as far as you are concerned. Look rather to what Christ is saying to you today: "My kingdom needs you. Therefore do not think of yourself as an outsider and do not let fear rule you." It is God's word that is calling you to be the living Church and the living voice of the Church. It does not leave you isolated. "Is this the springtime of your kingdom, Lord?"

It is also necessary that some, more than one, go out from the four walls of the house and, as Don Mazzolari has written, "pitch the tent of love alongside the tent of hatred, and take a position, openly, against all the cruelties of the day, whatever be the name behind which they hide, in an endeavor to promote a social holiness that will infuse a soul once more into this world of ours that has lost it." This is to be done more by one's life than by words, more through the word of life than by means of all the discussions. "Your word, Lord, desires to be heard, witnessed to, and proclaimed."

The Word that Saves

Dear brother or sister in the faith, the Lord does not ask exceptional oratorical powers of you, but great faith in and love for the word that saves. Your own words will then pour out without hesitation and will be convincing, persuasive, and overwhelming. You possess this word, you hear it within you; do not hug it to your bosom and keep it for yourself. Do not allow it to be smothered, even if you see distrustful eyes turned toward you, even those of a community that still has something of the authoritarian spirit in it or of brothers and sisters who are always ready with all their "buts" and "ifs." Make this word known. Try to speak it in your little world, in your community, and thus begin to put a somewhat stagnant faith in motion and to break the hard shell of apathy that exists everywhere to some extent.

This word is not to be spoken as if it were just another piece of news. It is Christ's word and the most unsettling word in human history. Do not forget this, lest you succumb to the danger of getting used to the word and trivializing it. This is the news that carries on the history of salvation every day in the events of the individual's life. This is why it is a word that demands commitment of us ourselves before we proclaim it, and a commitment so profound that we cannot but proclaim it. "This proclamation becomes the news of freedom, the great news of your freedom, O Christ."

What is catechesis, then, but the proclamation of the word of God made flesh? It is the gospel proclaimed to the people of today with its utterly disconcerting divine challenges to the evil in the present world, and proclaimed with love of a God who waits patiently for every sincere human quest of him and offers great hope amid all the suffering of the poor and afflicted. Dear brother or sister in the faith, you are delivering a proclamation of hope and freedom to the people of our day. Do not lose hope! Seek freedom in all its purity. Do not stop at the first flash of light: seek farther. You will see: Christ will not disappoint you; he is indeed the word that saves and sets free. This is the catechetical message people are most eagerly awaiting. Bring the expectations of people today face to face with the response of Christ. Do not betray these expectations with answers that are vague and short lived, merely improvised or routine. "My God, what an extraordinary mission this is! And yet you call all to it, provided they are believers enamored of your freedom."

Beloved, it is time for you to stir yourselves. Do not be afraid. Begin with a little and with a few people, without ever removing your gaze from the Spirit who educates. Catechists are not produced by improvisation. The word does not allow this. Catechesis is a journey of faith that requires its practicioners to be completely open to grace and docile to the Spirit of freedom. Then, too, catechists must not be too hurried and impatient. Catechesis advances at the pace set by the Spirit. It is God's great way that we should educate ourselves and others to be patient and to wait, to know how to grasp every point, or even a hint of one, at which human affairs and the mystery of Christ's word meet.

You must also be patient, very patient, with yourself: you are someone on the way, not someone who has arrived. The word you proclaim to your brothers and sisters cannot fail to involve you in crises, in order thereby to spur you to walk in even greater freedom and to draw your brothers and sisters along with you.

"Grant us, Lord, catechists who are mature and ready to serve your word with great generosity, while never tiring of listening to it in great and humble faith."

Il Segno 3 (March 1991)

Chapter 15

As I reflected upon how I might end this series of articles, I thought of something I had written many years ago: notes made in March 1974 for a series of conversations I was engaged in for Vatican Radio on the subject of evangelization. My study of the subject also involved research I did on evangelization in the very early Church in preparation for the 1973 meeting of the Italian Episcopal Conference, the purpose of which was to adopt and launch the theme of "Evangelization and the Sacraments."

Back to the Beginning

It was in that year that the themes of evangelization and mission acquired an official place in the planning of the Italian Episcopal Conference and, subsequently, in all aspects of pastoral action. Presently, as Bishop Renato Corti is succeeding Bishop Aldo Del Monte as Bishop of Novara, it is a pleasure to recall that at the 1973 meeting it was Bishop Del Monte who delivered a programmatic address on evangelization which is regarded as valid even today. My own reflections on the subject were set down in anticipation of that meeting, in which I too had been invited to participate. I have reviewed the notes I prepared for that meeting in order to compare them with the ideas I have been presenting in this series of articles for *Il Segno.* I am astonished at the agreement between ideas expressed at that time and the ideas expressed today. This indicates that the Italian Episcopal Conference was already on the mark.

Today, eighteen years later, we have to acknowledge that the path chosen was the proper one. In this article, therefore, I am repeating some of my insights from that year in order to give myself and my readers a chance to reflect a little on the road we have travelled and to catch our breath for the rest of our journey on the never-ending path of evangelization.

What Is Evangelization?

The reality to which the term *evangelization* points is an ancient one, but the word itself is recent. It is not found in the New Testament and is almost never used by the Fathers. It is worth noting that at least until the beginning of the 1970s the large theological dictionaries did not have an entry for evangelization. If we were to trace the recent origin of the word, we would probably find it first used in Protestant circles. Especially since the last century, evangelization has been a watchword for those groups of our Evangelical brothers and sisters that have committed themselves to the spread of the message and engaged in an intense proselytizing. This is one reason why the word has not always been warmly welcomed in all the Evangelical Churches, namely, that it suggested a particular way of spreading the gospel.

The Second Vatican Council used the word, even if only rarely. For example, in its decree on the laity, *Apostolicam actuositatem* the Council says, "The laity have very many opportunities for exercising the apostolate of evangelization and sanctification." Since the council, the word has been more frequently used in documents of the Catholic Church. For example, the Italian Episcopal Conference uses it in its 1970 document on the fundamentals of catechesis. It says, "Evangelization in the strict sense is the first proclamation of salvation to those who for various reasons do not yet know of it or do not yet believe." It goes on to say that evangelization can also accompany Christian life inasmuch as "even believing Christians always need to hear the proclamation of the truth regarding the fundamental facts of salvation" (no. 25). In regard to the conference's subsequent decision in 1973 to choose as its topic the promotion of a better understanding of the close connection between evangelization and the sacraments, the bishops themselves said that the choice was to be considered "not simply as an opportunity for giving a new impulse to pastoral activity" but "as a choice that focuses on the essentials of Christianity and suggests the concrete way in which the Church wants to operate effectively among people." But the most complete treatment of the subject is in Paul VI's encyclical *Evangelii nuntiandi* of 1975. In the recent encyclical, *Redemptoris missio,* of John Paul II, the word *evangelization* is repeated and applied to contemporary situations. But I have already discussed this in the preceding installment.

In the Very Early Church

There is one New Testament book that is expressly concerned with evangelization—the Acts of the Apostles. It tells of how the very early Church succeeded in a few years' time enthusiastically and courageously to evangelize all the countries between Syria and Greece. Acts provides valuable information on what the very early Church understood by "evangelization." To "evangelize" means, concretely, "to proclaim Jesus . . . saying, 'He is the Son of God'" (Acts 9:20); it means: to "testify to both Jews and Greeks about repentance toward God and faith toward our Lord Jesus" (Acts 20:21).

The early Church had, however, a great variety of formulas for use. From this is to be inferred that the reality behind the terminology was also a very rich one. Acts 17:1-3 sums up Paul's preaching by saying that he went about "explaining and proving that it was necessary for the Messiah to suffer and to rise from the dead"; he asserted, "This is the Messiah, Jesus, whom I am proclaiming to you." A like summary is given in Acts 26:22-23: Paul says, "nothing but what the prophets and Moses said would take place: that the Messiah must suffer, and that, by being the first to rise from the dead, he would proclaim light both to our people and to the Gentiles." As we reread the great sermons in Acts we see that they have at their center Jesus, his death and resurrection, and the salvific value of these events, along with a summons to conversion.

The content of the evangelization carried on by the very early Church can therefore be described as the proclamation of what God has done in the life, death, and glorification of Jesus Christ, who now offers the forgiveness of sins and the gift of the Spirit to anyone who heeds the proclamation and is converted. Evangelization in the very early Church was therefore the proclamation of a great event that has taken place, namely, the Christ event and its transforming results. Both of these elements are important. In fact, even when New Testament preaching dwells on the results of the transformation, it always relates these to the decisive Christ event. It is not some abstract value such as the primacy of poverty or the reversal of human situations, but the presence of Jesus among us that fulfills the promises of God. This is the foundation and permanent point of reference for all evangelization in the early Church.

By What Method?

What method did the very early Church use in evangelizing? Let me try to answer this question on the basis of the information given in the Acts of the Apostles. From this we learn that preachers always took the hearers into account when deciding the manner of proclaiming the good news. The message to be proclaimed was indeed the message of Christ, and even Christ himself. But the proclamation always took place in a particular context, namely, the relation between message and hearer. If we examine the discourses in Acts, we see that this context finds expression in the use of four important categories: *sign, Spirit, Scripture,* and *religious experience.* I shall briefly explain each of these four terms.

The relation to the hearer is often established by means of a *sign,* that is, a miracle. Something extraordinary happens (for example, the cure of the cripple in the temple) and then serves as the starting point for the proclamation of the risen Christ and for the summons to repentance. After the miraculous cure of the cripple (Acts 3), Peter says to the people, "You Israelites, why do you wonder at this, or why do you stare at us, as though by our own power or piety we had made him walk? The God of Abraham, the God of Isaac, and the God of Jacob, the God of our ancestors has glorified his servant Jesus, whom you handed over and rejected in the presence of Pilate, though he had decided to release him. But you rejected the Holy and Righteous One and asked to have a murderer given to you, and you killed the Author of life, whom God raised from the dead. . . . Repent, therefore, and turn to God so that your sins may be wiped out" (Acts 3:12-15, 19).

A second context is that of the *Spirit*, that is, the manifestations to which the gift of the Spirit gives rise in those who have believed. The presence of the Spirit is the sign that Christ is risen and has sent his Spirit as a gift to believers.

In some other instances, the context is the appeal to *Scripture*. When hearers accept the Old Testament as manifestation of a divine plan, the preacher starts with Old Testament passages and shows that the plan has been fulfilled in Jesus. Thus in Acts 17 we are told that Paul went to the synagogue in Thessalonica, "as was his custom," and "on three sabbath days argued with them from the Scriptures, explaining and proving that it was necessary for the Messiah to suffer and to rise from the dead; and saying, 'This [Jesus] is the Messiah'" (Acts 17:2-3).

In dealing with those who did not believe in the Scriptures, the preacher appealed to the general *religious experience* of the hearers. For example, Paul tells the pagans of Athens, You have achieved a religious understanding of the history of the world. I now announce to you that the fullness of this understanding is given to you in the risen Jesus: "What you worship as unknown, this I proclaim to you. The God who made the world and everything in it, he who is Lord of heaven and earth, does not dwell in shrines made by human hands. . . . While God has overlooked the times of human ignorance, now he commands all peoples everywhere to repent, because he has fixed a day" (Acts 17:23-24, 30-31).

It is worth noting here not only individual instances of contextualization of the word (the categories of sign, Spirit, Scripture, and religious experience), but also the fact that preaching in the course of evangelization ordinarily depends on a context. At a minimum, it depends on a communal context of lived Christianity. In his letters St. Paul speaks of "preaching with power"; I think that this "power" is to be understood not only as the display of extraordinary signs but also as the renewal of the community that accepts the message. The method of evangelization, then, ordinarily consists in an appeal to present reality and to a lived experience of the hearers.

The preeminent object of evangelization is the person of Jesus. Therefore every definition of the content of evangelization, as well as every new proposal of a way of evangelizing, must be judged by comparison with the reality as found in Christ the Lord. He is the perennial point of comparison. Consequently, all descriptions of the content of evangelization are insufficient if they refer only to a human situation which has been changed or is to be changed, while omitting any substantive reference to the Author of this change, namely, Christ, and to the transcendent character of the change, which is the work which God accomplishes through faith, repentance, conversion, and the gift of the Spirit. A sermon concerned solely with a human situation to be changed may be a philosophical and social sermon, but it is not evangelization, since it makes no substantive reference to him who changes the situation, namely, Jesus Christ, and to the transcendent character of the change, which consists not in a relation between a cause—which we introduce—and an effect—which we expect according to human norms—but in conversion, faith, acceptance of the evangelical rule of humility and peace, and the transforming gift of the Spirit.

Christ is also the reason for the proclamation. It is he who sends. The proclamation is a charge, a mission, a responsibility; it is also, therefore, a duty whose gravity depends on the kind of mission received. It is a duty for all baptized persons in general, and a duty in particular for all those on whom the

Church specifically lays this charge. Since it is a duty, it is not an easy task nor one that promises immediate satisfactions. It is a mandate that requires perseverance and fidelity. The seed in the gospel parable bears fruit through persevering patience.

Concluding Prayer

If the work of evangelization is not easy and does not yield immediate results, then we must sustain our patience and perseverance through prayer. For this reason, just as I began my letter, "Departure from Emmaus," with a prayer, so now I wish to end this series of articles with a prayer in which I join with all my readers:

"This evening, once again, darkness weighs upon my city, and the blaze of its inviting lights hides human worries and loneliness. And to make the setting even gloomier, alarming news comes from every side. But you, Lord, bid me look to you and to see every human event in you. Yes, in you, Christ, everything is set free in the abiding truth that puts every aggressive feeling, every hasty judgment, into perspective.

"We need your light, O Christ, and your way of judging with justice and love. Our hearts are already weighed down by their limitations and cannot bear the thought of heaven, too, being darkened by the hatreds of us mortals with our quick-sand hearts.

"'Stay with us because it is evening,' O Christ, and once again break this bread of yours. Then our clouded or weary eyes will be opened and will contemplate you in all created reality, even in the evening, when all is dark.

"Look, here we are, journeying to Jerusalem. The whole diocese is with me. At the breaking of bread we have left Emmaus behind and our fears and timidities as well; at the breaking of your bread, Christ, bread that when broken and given with faith and love will be able to satisfy the hunger of all humankind, for whether they are poor or rich in possessions, they are still in need of life-giving certainties. We are a journeying community, Lord. Be with us with your word that throbs within us with irresistible vitality. We are journeying, Lord, because this word of yours is a way of freedom. We cannot halt, for we would also halt your freedom and the journey through human history. We are journeying, Lord, because we want to bear witness to everyone that freedom is possible and that it cannot be broken up into countless evanescent ideals. For there is but one truth: the truth of a God crucified out of love, a God who is with us. We are journeying, O Christ, because we believe in the human beings whom you have redeemed, whom you love, and we believe in the light more than in the darkness. If this world were to recover a greater confidence in itself and were to work together, we would not be trembling here this evening or fearing dreadful nightmares and visions of death.

"Christ, you ask us for greater faith and courage, and you reassure us that this world of ours has unpredictable reserves, especially of goodness, and is like a shoot ready to break through hard soil that has been pounded down by hypocrisies of every kind. Here is where our mission is, Lord: the mission of disciples and believers who listen to your word and feel the attraction of your freedom. This world calls to us, Lord, because you call us to collaborate with you on this patch of earth, in order that your kingdom may come, here and everywhere.

"This evening I beg you once again, O Christ: break your bread anew and give your word to your believing disciples, your enthusiastic community, this waiting universe that seeks and hopes and dreams of authentic freedom. And the dream will come true through your boundless gift and the gift of our evangelical testimony."

"Holy Virgin, Mother of God, sweet creature ennobled by the Spirit of freedom, follow us with your generous, tender gaze on this hard pilgrimage of ours from mission to mission, and help us turn every thirsty soul into a redeemed soul. Amen."

Il Segno 4 (April 1991)